MW00637495

"In order to be irreplaceable,
one must always be different."

(Coco Chanel)

Text
Chiara Pasqualetti Johnson

Editorial Project
Valeria Manferto De Fabianis

Graphic Layout
Maria Cucchi

COCO CHANEL

REVOLUTIONARY WOMAN

WHITE STAR PUBLISHERS

Contents

Introduction   6

Gabrielle Bonheur Chanel, Better Known as Coco   12

31 Rue Cambon, The Dominion of Mademoiselle   48

The Return of the Queen   100

A Legendary Perfume   178

Fashion Fades, Only Style Remains the Same   196

Coco Chanel photographed by Man Ray in 1935. An iconic shot that encapsulates all the elements of her revolutionary style: the slender figure, the black dress, the ever-present hat, the real pearls, and the costume jewelry.

Introduction

A white tweed suit or an evening gown, wearing a brimmed hat or sometimes just a black hair bow, perfectly coiffed hair, a proud gaze, and a cascade of pearls around her slender neck. Impudent and regal, Coco was the perfect incarnation of the timeless elegance that made her immortal. The style she created was as simple as it was unmistakable; and although she never claimed to be a feminist, she created the modern woman and forever revolutionized the concept of femininity with her interpretation of the spirit of her times. Her clothes were easy to wear and easy to love. They gave a generation of women the freedom to roll up their own sleeves, in more ways than one. She pushed them to wear jackets that until then had only been a man's prerogative, symbolically guiding them toward their battle for independence, economic and otherwise. Coco Chanel represented (and dressed) a new generation of women, the ones who could pull off wearing trousers and who would be able to change the world with their tenacity, becoming masters of their own fate.

An elegant woman's attire had always confirmed her place in a world in which the freedoms granted to females were very limited. Long skirts, cumbersome hats, tight shoes, and high heels all made it difficult for them to walk and forced them to carry themselves like fragile objects in need of protection. Very few of them could choose the man they would marry, only a few had an income that they could dispose of as they saw fit, and none of them had the right to vote. All of this was unacceptable for a woman who refused social conventions and considered freedom to be a supreme asset. One snip of the scissors at a time, Coco Chanel cleared away all that was superfluous and began a revolution that leapt beyond the bounds of 19th-century femininity, freeing women of their corsets and crinolines to combine style and comfort. She decreed: "True elegance cannot disregard the convenience of moving freely."

The "freed" woman created by Coco moved with agility and nonchalance, even in her evening gowns. With no laces and no bustier, even a woman's posture became more relaxed. In ten years, she had revolutionized the female wardrobe, shortening skirts to below the knee, lowering waistlines, and inventing the *petite robe noire*, the little black dress that epitomized Parisian chic.

Coco Chanel photographed in 1936 by the portraitist of Paris's stars, Boris Lipnitzki, with her iconic six strands of pearls. She was superstitious and wore them both day and night, to ward off bad luck and to brighten the stark black of her garments.

Her "luxurious poverty"—made of essential shapes and few frills, but with extremely high-quality designs and fabrics—prevailed, swaying even those who had nostalgically held on to the past. There is a famous story from the era when the stylist Paul Poiret still dominated the fashion scene, dressing his clients in cascades of velvet in true Belle Époque style. It narrates a chance meeting between the two on a Parisian street. Seeing Coco, who was wearing what would become her legendary little black dress, Poiret sniggered and asked: "For whom are you in mourning, Mademoiselle?" A provocation, to which Coco replied: "For you, Monsieur." Rarely is the story of someone's life so deeply intertwined with the transformation of an era's awareness and evolution of style. As exciting as a novel, Coco Chanel's life story was one of records set. She was the first queen to ascend to the throne of the world of *haute couture*, which had always been dominated by men. One after the other, she launched the sailor style, jersey as a noble fabric, and then short jackets, gold buttons and low-waisted skirts, real pockets and fake jewelry. She created so much more than a way to dress—she pioneered a style. Driven by her rebellious spirit, her courage and resourcefulness, she lived a thousand lives, striding majestically through the 20th century, right up until the end. In 1910, she inaugurated her first milliner's shop in

Rue Cambon in Paris, an address that would become legendary, and imposed such decisive changes on the world of fashion that, from one day to the next, it leapt ahead a hundred years. Then she opened her second boutique in Deauville, a refined seaside location, and a third in the equally mundane Biarritz, where clients contended to own her designs, the symbol of the new elegance that she so brilliantly interpreted. The woman who had never even found the time to marry declared: "There is a time for work and a time for love. That leaves no other time." She dressed and worked like a man, proving better than any model could that with comfortable fashion, conceived to comply with the body and not to dominate it, she could achieve an androgynous look without ever losing grace or composure. Her style triumphed in the 1920s. She was already rich and famous, and her ambiguous charm grew with her new tomboy haircut, which was as much a hit as her designs. She started from nothing, but her acute business sense took her to the top as she transformed the Chanel fashion house into an empire that in 1936 had 3,800 employees, almost all of whom were women.

With her extraordinary capacity for observation, she was able to perceive nuances and details at each encounter, which she re-elaborated and transformed into something original. All of her loves and each of her friends left their trace in the Chanel style, at least as strong as the one she left in them. Although it may seem impossible, our idea of elegance is still influenced by a sentimental relationship from a century ago. As she dug through the wardrobes of her lovers, the charm of her innate French taste merged with her original fascinating ideas and enriched the Chanel style with elements that were destined to become legendary. Her first love, Boy Capel, taught her the beauty of simplicity, inspiring her to design the sporty, comfortable creations in jersey that would become her fortune. The grand duke Dmitri, grandson of Alexander II, refined the sense of opulence that she poured into her costume jewelry. The duke of Westminster made her fall in love with the coarseness of tweed, which she transformed into soft feminine jackets. She retreated from the scene when the war broke out; but at 71, exhausted by idleness, with a move worthy of a queen, she was back in the spotlight, astonishing the world as she challenged the New Look, and Christian Dior's full skirts, with the exquisite suits that all the stars would soon be wearing. In a year's time, she was once again riding the wave of success, ready to take back her place on the throne with her usual manner and a seemingly infinite series of genius intuitions that included her quilted bag and her two-tone slingbacks. "I don't regret anything in my life except the things I didn't do," said the woman who had done so, so many things. Was her life easy? Not at all. It would

be easy to be fooled by the shiny photos of her in her years of glory, triumphant after a successful fashion show or as she smiles alongside important friends; but Gabrielle Bonheur Chanel, Coco, survived dark periods and absolute pain that made the imaginative world she created a miracle. Before she became an icon in the world of fashion, praised the world over, she had been Gabrielle, a young girl abandoned at an orphanage. With tenacity and creativity she made it through the black hole of desperation, stubbornly sweeping away her past to create a legend. She never spoke the name of her ancestors' birthplace and never let anyone see her shed a tear about her abandonment by the reprehensible father that her imagination made into a hero.

Guided by her passionate nonconventionality, she sewed herself a future as though it were a dress, going from misery to myth. No one else has ever proven so firmly that style is not improvised: it must be cultivated with discipline, study, and passion, a lesson that Coco Chanel always followed with dedication and unfailing genius. "Time works for me," she used to say, and, as always, she was right. Her legend has made her immortal. She will go down in history as the revolutionary fashion icon that taught women the secret of timeless elegance and the way to feel free, confident, modern: but above all, unique. Because as Coco always said, "Fashion fades; only style remains the same."

"You can be gorgeous at thirty, charming at forty, and irresistible for the rest of your life."

A portrait from 1937, signed Horst P. Horst. At 54, Coco was at the height of her glory: still beautiful and immensely wealthy.

Gabrielle Bonheur Chanel, Better Known as Coco

From her humble origins to the creation of her brand. The dazzling ascent of the little girl raised in an orphanage began with a straw boater hat banded with a black ribbon and continued with the invention of Chanel N° 5, the first perfume to bear the name of a stylist. It was 1921, and the world of fashion would never be the same.

On a warm summer evening in 1883, the sun was casting pink reflections on the waters of the Loire as it lapped the banks in the little town of Saumur. Jeanne Devolle, who was just twenty-one, had a little girl named Julia and another on the way when she knocked on the door of the hospital run by the Sisters of Providence. Despite her contractions, she had waited until the last moment to leave home; as a result, it was in the admissions office that she delivered her second-born child, Gabrielle Bonheur. The child's father, Albert Chanel, was a carefree, womanizing street peddler who had no inclination for a traditional family, but Jeanne was so hopelessly in love with him that she followed him in his wanderings and even accepted the fact that their two children were born out of wedlock. Faced with scandal, Albert was forced to improvise a hasty wedding ceremony, but not before collecting a dowry from the young bride's family. A year later, their third child, Alphonse, was born, followed by Antoinette, Lucien, and ultimately little Augustin, who died in infancy.

One of the rare portraits of her in her youth, dated 1909. That year in Paris, Coco began producing the little straw hats that she signed using her real name, Gabrielle Chanel.

The family wandered continuously from one end of France to the other, following Albert, who was always looking for the best place to peddle cheap undergarments; but business was bad, and ensuring that the family was fed fell to Jeanne, who took a job as a washerwoman. Gabrielle's childhood was already full of sadness and poverty; but when her mother died, leaving her in the hands of a distant and rather unscrupulous father, it became tragic. Jeanne and Albert's sons were entrusted to a public assistance bureau, who placed them with local farming families, but the daughters were left in Albert's custody. He was forty at the time and he felt he still had a lifetime ahead of him that would be better spent without the hindrance of a family. He needed to get rid of his daughters, but where could he leave them? Albert's father, the grandfather of the little girls, was a prolific parent who already had 19 other children of his own, so he would certainly not be willing to take on the care of another two, and Jeanne's humble family lacked the resources to take them in. So it was that one morning in March, Albert set off towards Aubazine. This small village in the Nouvelle-Aquitaine region was built around an ancient abbey that was home to a girls' orphanage, and it was here that he abandoned Gabrielle and her sisters, sealing their fates forever. Looking back on that heart-wrenching moment, Gabrielle whispered "I was twelve. They'd taken everything away from me. I was dead. You can die more than once in your life." For her entire life, she battled the memory of her father's desertion, an abandonment that left wounds so deep, they would never heal. She often said that her pride was the only thing that saved her.

In the years that she spent within the grim walls of the convent, her only consolation came from the short vacations she was able to take at the home of her father's sister, Aunt Louise, who shared her frivolous passion for hats. Louise's original tastes could never be satisfied by the ordinary models sold in the small-town shops, so she had felt hats sent to her from Vichy; when they arrived, she cut and decorated them to suit her tastes. Gabrielle watched as Louise created; for the first time, she realized that the long hours that the nuns forced her to spend sewing could turn into something more than a boring pastime: they could become something creative, perhaps even a profession.

In 1902, when Gabrielle left the finishing school of Notre-Dame a Moulins where she had been living for two years, she was a small, olive-skinned girl with thick jet-black hair pulled back into a braid and an androgynous physique that had none of the generous curves that were admired at the time. She went to live with another of her father's sisters, Aunt Adrienne, who was only a year older than Gabrielle. They shared an attic room in a building on the outskirts of Moulins and worked together as clerks at the Maison Grampayre, a company specializing in tailor's supplies that had two display windows in the Rue de l'Horologe, in the center of town. Gabrielle soon learned her way around fabrics, slips, veils, and fur collars; before long, she was giving expert advice to the most demanding customers, who trusted her tastes when they placed their orders and her handiwork when they needed small alterations done. After work, in her attic room, Gabrielle began sewing dresses and skirts for them to give a small boost to her modest salary; for the first time in her life, she was able to indulge in a few evenings out at the Rotonde, one of the town's *café-chantants* frequented by officers of the garrisons stationed in Moulins. She was fascinated by this dazzling scene and, on a whim, she decided to offer her services as a *poseuse*, joining the ranks of the attractive "fake spectators" who performed in the intervals between acts.

Gabrielle with her Aunt Adrienne in Vichy in 1906. Both are wearing dresses and hats that they had made themselves, the first Chanel designs of which there is a photo.

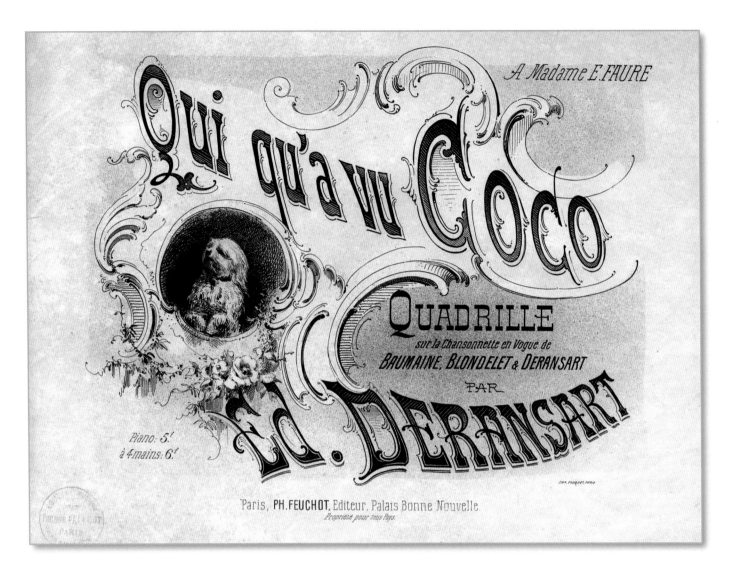

Qui qu'a vu Coco

J'ai perdu mon pauvr' Coco,
Coco mon chien que j'adore,
tout près du Trocadéro
Il est loin s'il court encore.
Je l'avoue, mon plus grand r'gret
Dans ma perte su cruelle,
C'est qu'plus mon homme me
trompait...
Plus Coco m'etait fidèle!

Vous n'auriez pas vu Coco?
Coco dans l'Trocadero
Co dans l'Tro
Co dans l'Tro

Coco dans l'Trocadero
Qui qu'a qui qu'a vu Coco?
Eh! Coco!
Eh! Coco!
Qui qu'a qui qu'a vu Coco?
Eh! Coco!

Pauvr' Coco que j'aimais tant
Il était victime d'un crime
Messieurs plaignez mon tourment
Car il est bien légitime
J'ai beau crier, le chercher
D'la Bastille à l'hyppodrome
J'lai partout fait afficher

je ne ferais pas ça pour mon homme
Vous n'auriez pas vu Coco?
Coco dans l'Trocadero
Co dans l'Tro
Co dans l'Tro
Coco dans l'Trocadero
Qui qu'a qui qu'a vu Coco?
Eh! Coco!
Eh! Coco!
Qui qu'a qui qu'a vu Coco?
Eh! Coco!

Gabrielle loved to sing and despite her lack of talent, the public found a particular fascination with her. Her repertoire was limited to three or four short, simple songs; successful catchy tunes like *Ko Ko Ri Ko* and *Qui qu'a vu Coco?* To encourage her to sing, her admirers chanted out syllables from the songs, Ko-Ko and Co-Co, and unwittingly assigned her the legendary nickname she would be known by for the rest of her life.

Years later, the memory of those difficult years and the humiliation she suffered when her employers discovered she was working as a singer led her to invent a more romantic origin for her nickname. She preferred to attribute it to her father, saying he called her "my little Coco." That allowed her to erase the sad reality of her childhood as an orphan, the years spent sewing in her attic in Moulins, and, above all, the memory of that loathsome father who had abandoned his daughter at such a tender age.

The musical score of the song "Qui qu'a vu Coco?" It was her pièce de résistance *when she performed at the* café-chantant *in the little town of Moulins.*

Among Coco's many admirers, one was particularly ardent. His name was Étienne Balsan, and, although he was a simple noncommissioned officer, he came from a rich bourgeois family that owned one of the most important textile factories in France. He transmitted his great passion for horses to his lover and in due time, persuaded her to move to the large estate, the Chateau de Royallieu, that he had purchased in 1904 with the intention of making it into a thoroughbred-breeding farm. At the time, Étienne had no idea that he was giving Gabrielle her first taste of what would become her most precious asset, her freedom. In no time, Coco's tenacity and strong will made her an expert equestrian; and at the same time, her wits and spirit won over the hearts of Étienne and the small circle of his wealthy friends who were regular guests at the

estate. She decided that, for her gallops through the forest, she needed riding attire that was more suitable than the cumbersome skirts that impeded her movements. She never imagined how revolutionary her gesture was when she asked the humble tailor in Croix-Saint-Ouen to sew her a pair of custom-made riding pants, identical to the jodhpurs that she had borrowed from an English groom. At the time, no woman would have dreamed of wearing anything of the kind. She often spoke about the episode, recalling the tailor's surprise, as well as her own surprise when he wrote to her in the 1930s, after recognizing her in a photograph.

Scandalously impeccable in her jockey garb, Coco shocked everyone with attire that became progressively simpler and more comfortable: men's shirts, neckties stolen from the closet of her host, capes made of raw wool, and simple straw boaters that she banded with ribbons herself. Her hat designs moved further and further away from the reigning opulence of the Belle Époque, as she asked herself "How can a brain function under those things?" Her style was already unique, made of the elegance and clean lines that characterized every thread of her garments.

Right: Gabrielle riding a horse alongside Boy Capel. She was wearing the daring pants that she had had made by the local tailor, patterned on a pair of jodhpurs she borrowed from one of the grooms.

In the small photo at the top: Gabrielle in riding gear with Léon de Laborde and Étienne Balsan in front of the stables at Royallieu.

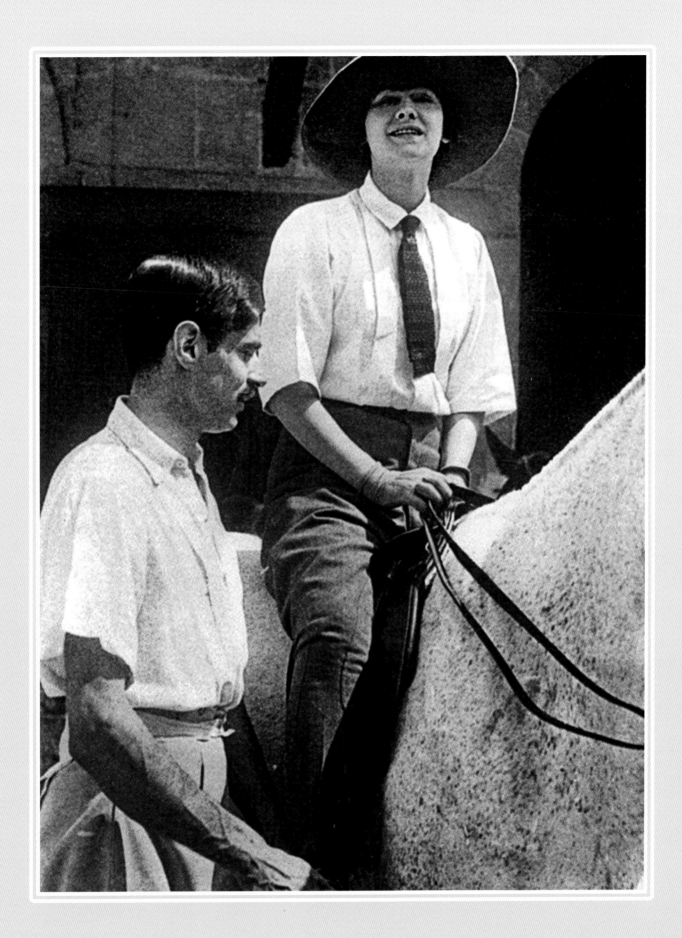

Boy Capel, reading in his bachelor's apartment in the Boulevard Malesherbes in Paris, where Chanel inaugurated her first milinery atelier in 1910.

The simple and somber hats she made were different from all others; they won the enthusiastic approval of Étienne's friends, so she began to create a few for them as well, to break up the monotony of life at Royallieu.

At age twenty-six, her future seemed to be less certain than ever, since she was completely dependent on the benevolence of Étienne, who had been supporting her and whose guest she had been for two years. She was grateful for his generosity, but her gratitude did not prevent her from falling head over heels in love with a pale-skinned, dark-haired English man who was introduced to her by none other than Étienne himself. His real name was Arthur Capel, but everyone called him Boy; and despite his unknown origins, he was regularly in the company of the best-known names of France's aristocracy. At thirty years old, he had made a rather decent fortune for himself, investing in coal mines. "Not a word was exchanged, only looks," she recalled.

Boy and Gabrielle on the beach at Saint-Jean-de-Luz, near Biarritz. Seen from the back is the sugar tycoon Constant Say.

Coco was young and in love, but she never lost sight of her goal of independence. "I'm following the path that I've chosen. I'm not a slave, because I chose it freely. I'm as strong as a bull and I've never missed one hour of work, I've never been sick," she repeated. She was true to these convictions her whole life. She now had everything she needed to begin building her future: great determination and a strong man she could lean on, a companion who could show her affection, trust, and respect but who could also teach her to look beyond the limits of her world. Capel was full of intellectual curiosity: he was interested in politics and history, an avid reader of Nietzsche and Voltaire; he devoured Herbert Spencer's political essays and Sully's *Mémoires*, which he insisted that Coco read as well. A few months after they first met, Boy took her to Paris and chose a house for them on the Champs-Élysées. Coco delighted in decorating it with luxurious pieces of furniture she found as she wandered from one Paris antique shop to another; and it was then that she bought the first of over thirty precious, black-lacquered Coromandel screens, decorated with gold, that would become one of her greatest passions.

Étienne also helped Coco turn her life around when, in the spring of 1909, he let her use his elegant *garçonnière* in the Boulevard Malesherbes so she could set up a small atelier and begin selling her hats.

Of course, her first customers were the rich and influential friends of Étienne whom she had met at Royallieu. They were excited by Coco's courage, and they were curious to see her creations, which were so much more solemn and original than the enormous hats that other Parisian milliners were designing. Thanks to their word of mouth, Coco's business increased enough to allow her to hire two workers and the prominent milliner Lucienne Rabaté. In October 1910, after two of her hats were featured in the pages of the magazine *Comœdia Illustré*, she decided to take a giant step. With some economic help from Boy, she rented a shop in the most elegant area of Paris, near the Opéra, a second-floor apartment in the Rue Cambon at an address that was destined to become almost as legendary as she herself was. The plaque near the door that read "Chanel Modes" engraved in block letters would become her trademark. As she proudly observed her name, printed black on white, she began to envision the two interlocking "C"s that would become the brand's logo. In her memoirs, she explained that the initials came from her past. One of her father's ancestors, an artisan from Ponteils, used them to brand the furniture he built, and they were reminiscent of the stain-glassed windows of the orphanage in Aubazine as well. But perhaps they were simply the initials of the name fate had given her, Coco Chanel.

In October 1910, two of Chanel's hat designs were published for the first time, in the Comœdia Illustré, *a Parisian magazine that specialized in theater chronicles and society news.*

Photo Félix.

Deux Créations de Gabrielle Chanel   Photo Félix.
21, rue Cambon, Paris

qui lui en sont faites. Que nous réserve-t-il pour la ville et le théâtre ? C'est ce que nous saurons bientôt....

❧

« Marie-Louise » nous donne un de ses modèles à la ligne savamment étudiée, inspiré des toiles anciennes où l'artiste puise le plus souvent ses créations si admirées. Celui-ci rappelle un célèbre portrait de Lawrence, que possède la «National Gallery».

❧

« Ida-Margueritte » nous montre une toque orignale, d'une forme ravissante et inédite, où se retrouve le cachet si parisien de la maison.

Les étoiles de l'Opéra-Comique s'y ren-

leurs comptoirs, mais ils y ajoutent l'étude de la ligne, et leurs vêtements sont d'une exécution parfaite et d'une riche élégance.

❧

« Lewis » fait une rentrée brillante; partout à la fois, cet homme est mondial.

Mlle Parys, la gracieuse Marcelle de *l'Enlèvement des Sabines*, nous montre, en couverture de ce numéro, un turban or, d'une richesse suggestive, surmonté d'un paradis incomparable au pied duquel brille un rubis étincelant.

Des deux chapeaux ci-contre, le marquis est d'une note jeune et charmante, et le petit chapeau de velours s'orne d'une plume d'autruche artistement posée en aigrette qui coiffe à ravir la jolie artiste.

❧

Le sac « Maquet » réapparaît aux mains de l'élégante Mlle Guerra. Ce sac est en broché de soie tons anciens, et accompagne la riche toilette que revêt l'artiste sur cette jolie photo. Ce sac est tout indiqué pour les robes habillées, et Maquet ne peut suffire aux commandes contrent chaque jour, en ce moment, et les salons sont envahis par la clientèle mondaine. On travaille ferme chez Ida-Margueritte.

Paris became deserted in the summer when the *beau monde* of the capital left the city to invade the most exclusive seaside resorts, such as Deauville. It was here in 1913, in the Rue Gontaut-Biron, the most elegant street in the city, that Boy persuaded Coco to open a new boutique. It was nestled between the Casino and the Normandy Hotel, shaded by a beige striped awning with her name in black letters. In addition to the hats that had already made her famous, she proposed articles that she had designed for her own personal wardrobe: jockey-style jerseys, sailor-style shirts that could be worn without a corset, and knit capes that were perfect for Deauville's holiday lifestyle. Her new pieces were met with the approval of important clients like the Baroness Rothschild, who ordered dozens of them and suggested the Chanel atelier to her wealthy friends, including a star of the French theater, Cécile Sorel. Her enormous success was crowned by an article in *Les Modes* that included full-page photos of her designs, modeled by the actress Gabrielle Dorziat and the singer Geneviève Vix. Coco and Boy were the most talked-about couple of the moment—and in fact, in one of his famous illustrations, the caricaturist and judge of elite elegance Sem (pseudonym of Georges Goursat) portrayed Coco hugging Boy, a polo-playing centaur, with one of her enormous hatboxes dangling from her arm. Opening the new boutique proved to be an even more long-sighted choice when Germany declared war on France on August 3, 1914. Parisians fled the city for the hotels and villas of Normandy, and among them were some of the most elegant women in France. When they arrived in Deauville, they found only one shop open, Coco's. Her simple casual style was perfectly suited to the solemn tastes imposed by the conflict, and her singular combination of masculine-inspired pieces with more traditional feminine ones came to be emblematic of her style.

Coco and Boy in a satirical illustration by Sem (pseudonym of Georges Goursat) from Le vrai et le faux chic, *the 1914 cartoon album he dedicated to the stars of Deauville society.*

One year later, Coco appeared in a photo taken on the beach of Biarritz, where she had rented a villa in front of the Casino and made it the new home of Chanel fashion on the Basque coast. It was a brilliant idea that brought her an even more resounding success than the one she enjoyed in Deauville.

She soon had sixty seamstresses working full-time to fill the orders that were arriving from France and Spain. In 1915, *Harper's Bazaar* wrote "The woman who hasn't got at least one Chanel is hopelessly out of fashion." A winning factor in her first collections was the introduction of handmade, industrially sewn knit fabric into the world of *haute couture*. From the outset,

Coco understood the array of sartorial possibilities that tricot could offer; and in 1916, Rodier, a resourceful French textile producer, gave her the exclusive rights to a supply of jersey, the new machine-made fabric that had been previously used only to make men's undergarments. Inspired by the freedom of sportswear, she created a collection of daywear that was simple and comfortable. It included simple sheath dresses and three-piece outfits with a skirt, a pullover, and a cardigan. These were just the kinds of pieces women wanted to put on when they came home from a formal occasion and they could finally be relaxed and at ease after hours of discomfort in a tight-fitting corset.

Chanel's new designs appeared in *Harper's Bazaar* in an article that featured her unstructured three-quarter-length jersey jackets with V-necks that left the neck daringly bare, worn over original masculine vests. As skirts became shorter and revealed feet, ankles, and even a bit more, newspapers reported that "Women's bodies haven't been covered using so little fabric since the era of the Greeks."

In one stroke, the new styles erased the centuries-old gesture of a woman discreetly pulling up the hem of her dress each time she went up a step. These dresses were destined for a new generation of women—women who played golf and drove cars and who, after the war broke out and the men left for the battlefront, managed important companies. The women who wore her dresses outshined the others, who looked older and more matronly in comparison. Chanel asserted that "Nothing makes a woman look older than obvious expensiveness and complication, and all those pleats."

On the eve of World War I in Deauville, Coco is wearing one of her designs made with a new fabric, jersey. The machine-knit material was considered too supple and had previously been used only to make undergarments for men.

On the facing page: Coco is playing golf in one of the new jersey Chanel outfits and a black straw hat.

Later, when the air-raid sirens forced Parisians to run for shelter in the dead of the night, Coco revolutionized her clients' nightwear as well, creating elegant white and burgundy satin pajamas that would allow them to maintain their impeccable appearance, even in such a dramatic situation.

When the war was over, fashion magazines took Chanel's fame to new heights in the United States—in fact, American women came to constitute a great part of her clientele. Her newly earned international recognition coincided with the opening of a new headquarters in Paris, in the Rue Cambon 31, just a short distance from her old atelier. It was in these new dazzling showrooms that Coco's character began to emerge, not only her volcanic creativity but the angry outbursts that terrified her employees as well. The arrival of "Mademoiselle," as they called her, was always a source of panic for the seamstresses and tailors; so when they saw her approaching, from the windows that faced the street, they immediately ran to their stations.

After the end of World War I, the Chanel style triumphed, leaping over the 19th-century idea of femininity in one bound. In the photo on the left, Coco is posing like a model in a white silk evening gown. On top: a silk overcoat with a fur collar and borders, a creation from one of her first collections.

"I was the same age
as the new century,
so it turned to me for
its expression in clothing.
What was needed was
simplicity, comfort,
neatness: unwittingly,
I offered all of that.
True successes are
destiny."

An intense close-up of Coco in the early 1920s, wearing a flashy bracelet
decorated with fake stones, one of her first pieces of costume jewelry,
which enhanced the simplicity of her white dress.

Chanel

Etheldra

Chanel's new jersey dresses appeared in the magazine Les Elégances Parisiennes *in 1917. On the facing page, a creation from the summer of 1917, in silk jersey embroidered in lacquer red. Its low waistline was accentuated with a soft belt draped around the hips.*

The choice of neutral colors like gray and black underlined the revolutionary elegance of this 1919 Chanel suit with a fur-bordered cape over a softly shaped sheath dress with fringes.

Appearing for the first time in this fall 1920 creation were pockets, a decorative but functional element that was destined to become a recurring style in her designs.

Coco lived with Boy in their house on the Champs-Élysées, just a stone's throw from where she worked. For years, she had been telling herself "Choose who you want to be, and become that woman," and ultimately that is what she was able to do. She had finally saved enough money to fully repay the loan he had made her years earlier—the loan that had made it possible for her to open her atelier and to become the woman she wanted to be, free and independent. He adored her, but he was an extremely ambitious man and he had a score to settle with his past, the bane of his humble origins. He knew that if he wanted to maintain his role in high society, he would need an aristocratic wife, so he singled out the daughter of a lord, Diana Lister. He continued his affair with Coco even after he was married, but the forced secrecy of their relationship grew more and more uncomfortable for her. Obviously they could no longer live together, so she moved into a rented apartment at the Alma, an eccentric residence with a mirror-covered bedroom, black-lacquered ceilings, and an enormous Buddha in the entryway. It was a style that left an indelible mark in her memory, one that would become a precious source of inspirations for her future dwellings. Coco felt suffocated by her solitude in Paris; so, when Boy announced the birth of his daughter, she decided to leave the city for La Milanaise, a quiet Paris suburb, in the hopes of numbing her pain. She rented a villa surrounded by a large estate where her two dogs, Soleil and Luna, lived, and bought a blue Rolls Royce with a black interior, a combination that was so unusual at the time that she launched a new trend for dark-colored cars. Her next residence, Villa Bel Respiro in Garches, was even more sumptuous. She moved there with her butler, her governess, and her beloved dogs who, in the meantime, had had a litter of five puppies that she named collectively Ursa Major. Set on a hill, the villa was painted beige with black shutters, a color combination Coco loved. She nicknamed it "Noix de Coco" and hosted a lively entourage of guests there, including Henry Bernstein and his wife Antoinette and daughter, who appears in a photo, hand in hand with Coco, smiling under a cloche hat that was far too big for her. Bernstein was taken by Coco's charms, and there were unconfirmed rumors of a brief affair between them.

At the end of 1919, the death of Boy Capel marked the end of an era for Coco. She would mourn him forever, grateful for the support he had offered at the beginning of her career and for the love of books he had instilled in her.

Coco Chanel on the beach at the Venice Lido, sitting next to her friend Misia Sert, dressed in white at the center of the photo.

Before Christmas 1919, there was a lot of gossip about Boy's failed marriage. He was reportedly separated from his rich English wife and ready to move back to France to be with the love of his life, Coco; but what appeared to be the coronation of their passion ended in tragedy. On December 22, as he was traveling to Monaco, he lost control of his car on an icy road and hit a tree and died. Coco, who was 37 years old, grieved: "It was a terrible blow for me. In losing Capel, I lost everything." After Boy's death, she was bereaved of any energy and desperately latched on to the affection of Misia Sert, who, she declared years later, was "the only friend I have ever had." There was always friction between the two, but they stayed loyal to each other until the end, inspiring each other and sharing a common passion for art that would condition the existence of both. Misia was the daughter of a Polish sculptor and lived in a world inhabited by painters, musicians, and poets. She was a friend of Mallarmé and Satie and the muse of Toulouse-Lautrec, who depicted her as a skater in a beautiful poster for *La Revue Blanche* in

1895. She also posed for Félix Vallotton, Vuillard, and Bonnard, as well as for Renoir, who was obsessed by her décolletage and painted her a number of times. She was the witness at the wedding of her friend Pablo Picasso, and was the godmother of his first child. Ravel dedicated two compositions to her, *Le Cygne* and *La Valse*. Misia opened the doors to a new world for Coco, the world of art, and introduced her to the most important players on Paris's avant-garde cultural scene, including Cocteau, Salvador Dalí, Picasso, and Satie. As she sat silently next to her friend, listening to the spirited debates between Diaghilev and Stravinsky about their latest works, she began to understand the complicated mechanisms of artistic creation. It was a lesson she would never forget, and she was eternally grateful to her friend for it. "Without Misia, I'd be an idiot," she humbly confessed to the French journalist Marcel Haedrich.

In her memoirs, Misia describes the first time they met, during a dinner organized by Cécile Sorel in 1917. "At the table, my attention was immediately drawn to a young woman with very dark hair who I found irresistibly charming, even though she didn't say a word. As soon as I finished eating, I found a way to go and sit next to her." Curiosity tuned into friendship in the summer of 1920, when they traveled together to Venice. There, surrounded by the decadent atmosphere of the city, Coco rediscovered a taste for living. With the exuberant Catalan painter José-Maria Sert, Misia's third husband, as her guide, she avidly took in every detail. He dragged her from one museum to the next and then to buy up troves of antiques, instilling a passion in her that would prove to be useful when she was selecting the furnishings for her domain in the Rue Cambon. In the evening, she sat at the Café Florian, exhausted and immersed in the silence of the surrounding churches. In a photo taken with Misia at the Lido, dressed in white with her ever-present straw hat, she seems to have found her smile again. For Coco, Venice became a place of revival, the city of mystery and wonder, of magic and symbols, starting with the lion that dominated Saint Mark's square, the animal that represented her zodiac sign and that would become her good-luck charm.

Surrounded by the cosmopolitan atmosphere of Venice, she began to assimilate every drop of the eccentric glamor she found in the masquerade balls and decadent nobility that carried the scent of the Orient. There, she met fascinating strangers with exciting pasts, like the grand duke Dmitri Pavlovich. He was a cousin of Tsar Nicholas II but had been exiled as one of the instigators of Rasputin's assassination, a punishment that saved him, just barely, from the Russian Revolution. He was eleven years Coco's junior, but she was won over by his pale, romantically heroic face and began a relationship with him that lasted less than a year in 1921, a year that would turn out to be fundamental for the future of Chanel. The affair ended without drama when he decided to offer his hand and his blazoned name to a rich young American heiress who possessed everything but a noble title. His marriage had no effect on the sincere friendship between Coco and the grand duke, and in fact it lasted until his death in 1942.

Life with the grand duke revolutionized Coco's style. When Dmitri was there, dinners in Villa Bel Respiro lasted into the small hours of the morning; and in the company of Igor Stravinsky and his artist friends, Russian was more frequently spoken than French. "There was never a dull moment with those people. Thank god, they never spoke of art, they simply *made* art, which is not the same thing," Coco said. When she found out that Stravinsky was experiencing serious economic difficulties, she invited him to live in the villa with his wife and four children. For two years, the house was filled with the notes of *Pulcinella*, the opera Stravinsky was able to orchestrate in that period, thanks to the generosity of his host.

Influence from the East also reached the atelier in the Rue Cambon. Ranks of downfallen princesses and impoverished countesses fled to Paris from Russia, including Dmitri's sister, Maria Pavlov. Coco was influenced by a vein of exoticism that became part of her collections and hired embroiderers, clerks and models. Coats and capes were decorated with colorful embroideries inspired by Russian folklore; the shape of overcoats was evocative of the military frock coat, the *pelisse;* and blouses were cinched with belts that resembled those worn by the Russian peasants, the *muzhik*. All this was in perfect harmony with the unequivocal simplicity that characterized the brand.

But the time she spent with Dmitri resulted in an even more resounding influence. During the summer of 1920, at the dawn of their romance, they took a trip to Grasse, where he introduced her to Ernest Beaux, a Moscow-born French chemist who had worked for years in the court of the tsar in St. Petersburg. There in Grasse, in the fragrant, blooming fields of Provence, the idea of creating a perfume for the Chanel brand was born. Other fashion houses had tried before her, but had obtained only disappointing results. Scents with evocative names like "*Lucrèce Borgia*" or Poiret's "*Nuits de Chine*" were produced according to tradition, using only natural essences, but Beaux encouraged Coco to experiment with aldehydes, a new synthetic substance that exalted the light powdery notes of the essences and

made the scent last longer on the skin. Over the course of 1921, Beaux sent her two series of samples and asked her to choose her favorite. They were numbered from 1 to 5 and from 20 to 24 and were composed of a variety of combinations of about eighty ingredients, the most prevalent of which were jasmine and rose, together with a massive dose of aldehydes. Coco had no doubts: she placed all her bets on Number 5.

Top: Ernest Beaux, perfumer of the tsars, in 1921 made a series of blends for Coco, among which was the blend for N° 5. Later he made other perfumes for Chanel, including N°22 and Cuir de Russie.

On the facing page: Coco and the grand duke Dmitri Pavlovich, the cousin of Tsar Nicholas II, in 1920 at the time of their relationship.

This was a perfume with no well-known notes or identifiable bouquet. Rather, it was evocative of soap, perhaps the one that Gabrielle remembered smelling on her mother's skin after she did laundry, combined with something provocative and sensual that made it unique. "A woman's perfume that smells like a woman" was exactly what she wanted, the essence of femininity, not the scent of flowers. Coco clarified: "I'm not looking for the smell of roses or lily of the valley; I want an elaborate perfume." Beaux said he had been inspired by "the marvelous, fresh breeze that comes off the waters of the lakes and rivers under the midnight sun" and had recreated a sensation he had experienced while on an expedition to the North Pole during the war.

The perfume's packaging was a revolutionary change from the usual fanciful, over-decorated bottles like those of Lalique and Baccarat. Coco, who loved simplicity and rigor, insisted on using a pharmacy bottle, a simple, transparent, rectangular prism, reminiscent of cubist art, with a diamond-cut stopper that was inspired by the geometric shape of Place Vendôme. The same taste for simplicity dictated the design of the label—a white rectangle with austere black letters like those used by avant-garde artists.

The only thing left was to choose a name for her new perfume. Since her fashion house was already famous, she decided to take advantage of that notoriety and baptize it simply as Chanel. But with her usual long-sightedness, she decided it was best to distinguish it from other possible perfumes that she might want to launch in the future; and since she had chosen sample number five, why not Chanel N° 5?

The revolutionary simplicity of the Chanel N° 5 bottle. Its rectangular shape with rounded corners and emerald-cut stopper were inspired by cubist sculptures.

Je le déclare sans vergogne
Il n'y a rien de moins Coco
Qu'une toilette de Coco
Parfumée à l'eau de Coco...
De Coco... de Cocologne

Marquise de la Flaconnerie

"Perfume is the unseen but unforgettable, ultimate fashion accessory. It heralds a woman's arrival and prolongs her departure."

Everything was ready for the launch of her perfume, but she shrewdly decided not to make it available for purchase immediately. Instead, she gave it as a gift to her most elegant friends, counting on their word of mouth, which did indeed turn out to be a powerful method of marketing. She prophetically announced: "I've chosen to launch my perfume on May 5, 1921, the fifth day of the fifth month of the year, and let that number bring me luck," and bring her luck it did. As soon as the precious essence was officially released, exclusively at her atelier at 31 Rue Cambon, clients snapped it up. The first batches were made by Rallet, a small Provencal producer where Ernest Beaux worked that also supplied the Russian court, but Coco was not satisfied with their work. Many bottles were defective and, more importantly, Rallet was unable to fill the increasing numbers of orders in the timeframe she demanded, so she decided to take her business to the brilliant owners of the cosmetic company Bourjois, the Wertheimer brothers, Pierre and Paul, whom she had met in Deauville. Together, in 1942, they founded the Société des Parfums Chanel in which Gabrielle and Pierre Wertheimer were partners and Ernest Beaux was the operations manager. Although she was an astute calculator, she had no notions of budgets, she quickly became bored with accounts and balance sheets and she hated being forced to think like a businesswoman. So the agreement stated that Coco would not be involved in the administrative or commercial management of the perfume; instead, she would simply receive 10% of the profits, an income that she would enjoy for the rest of her life and that would always shield her from hardship.

A tribute to the Chanel perfume in a 1923 drawing by Sem, with an inscription for Coco that read "Marchioness of the bottle," and her caricature, framed by the unmistakable N° 5 bottle.

As she became more and more captivated by the world of perfumes, Coco fell in love with a flower from Japan that reminded her of an event that took place in her childhood. She was just thirteen when she saw Sarah Bernhardt's rendition in the theater production of Dumas's novel *La Dame aux Camélias* (The Lady with the Camellias), a performance that moved her to tears. In that period, the camellia that Dumas had glorified was blazoned as a lapel flower adorning the jackets of Marcel Proust and the dandies of his day. Once again, Coco dipped into the world of men's attire to appropriate that candid white, long-blooming flower and used it to illuminate her creations, pinning one to a chiffon dress for the first time in 1923.

Since then, the camellia has been ever-present, in every collection and in an infinity of variations—in fabric or precious stones, embroidered on the neckline of her dresses, delicately set on belts or on the lapels of her suit jackets, as a hair ornament, and often transformed into a piece of jewelry. They were produced by artisans such as those of the historic atelier Lemarié, which was founded in 1880 and today is the only plumassier left that is still capable of transforming feathers into jewels. Over the years, Chanel paid such homage to the camellia in pins, bags, dresses, and hats that the flower became a symbol of the Chanel brand. Its simple geometry suits the Chanel style perfectly, and, since it has no scent, it will never be in competition with a woman's personal choice of perfume—ideal for anyone who, like Coco, thinks that "a woman must wear perfume wherever she wants to be kissed."

One of the symbols of the Chanel fashion house was the camellia. Pure white with a perfect geometric structure, it was used to decorate accessories and gowns like this black and white creation that appeared in Vogue *magazine in 1927.*

31 Rue Cambon, The Dominion of Mademoiselle

The Chanel style revolution. In the Parisian atelier where Coco Chanel worked and lived, icons were created that would revolutionize the concept of feminine elegance. Her little black dress, her costume jewelry, and her striped tops with gold buttons were all a breath of fresh air that would blow from Paris to Hollywood.

Her character, verve, and sharp sense of irony made Coco a fascinating creature in her time, and her atypically slim figure, rather than diminishing her allure, made it unique. With her impeccable taste in shapes, colors, and fabrics, she succeeded in beautifully accentuating her lithe physique. She never went unnoticed, and everything she wore became a model for others to imitate, including the white, baggy pajama-style trousers that she publicized with a photo of herself, tanned and on vacation. Her suntan, emphasized by a cascade of pearls, would set a trend, and salons all over Paris were hard-pressed to keep up with the demands for her tomboy style when she decided to freshen her image and cut her magnificent hair. She had been wearing her thick, black, waist-length hair in three braids coiled around her head, when she decided to try a daring cut that would reveal the long neck that she prided herself on. In her memoirs, the tale of that bold act became part of the repertoire of classic Chanel anecdotes. With a touch of imagination, she liked to narrate how, as she was leaving to go to the Opera, the water heater exploded and ruined her hairstyle, so she was forced to cut it off.

One of Chanel's iconic looks was pure white wide-legged trousers, a cascade of pearls on a dark sweater, and a sailor cap. Here she is seen posing at the Venice Lido with Marcello Caracciolo, duke of Laurino.

Coco Chanel wearing a sailor-style top and jersey trousers, surrounded by lavender at Villa La Pausa on the French Riviera. At her feet is her dog, Gigot.

Regardless of whether her tale was legend or truth, her choice created a sensation and a long-lasting style that would launch a new type of woman, the type celebrated in Victor Margueritte's scandalous, best-selling novel, *La Garçonne*. The novel's heroine was a woman with a tomboy cut who was financially independent, nonchalant in choosing her lovers, and exaggeratedly emancipated for her times, just like Coco. Everyone copied her haircut and wore a cloche like hers down over their eyes.

In the meantime, the lines of Chanel dresses became more and more fluid, waistlines disappeared, and curvaceous women had to resort to binding their breasts with Velpeau bandages to achieve a taller, slimmer silhouette. Coco made them all look like her.

In the 1920s, the androgynous style launched by Coco achieved unprecedented success, and Paris was its stage. The pages of the era's magazines demonstrate the influence that the Chanel style had on fashion; publications like *Minerva* and *Femina* were practically catalogs of her creations. In that period, Coco added what would become another classic of the Chanel style to her dresses: pockets, a feature typical of work clothes, which would free women from the hindrance of carrying a purse all the time.

In a pair of men's-style trousers, Coco is seen posing between the set designer Christian Bérard and the dancer Boris Kochno in Monte Carlo in 1932.

The simple, soft lines achieved with an innovative use of jersey characterized Chanel's designs in the late 1920s. Her usual strands of pearls and a collar of white piqué brightened her outfit, and a black straw hat completed the look.

Coco Chanel photographed by Berenice Abbott as she shows off the new tomboy haircut that would be imitated by millions of women and complemented by comfortable knit outfits in natural colors, such as this pleated wool jersey skirt.

Coco, posing in the garden of her Faubourg-Saint-Honoré home in May 1929, wearing a knit skirt and cardigan. The capacious pockets were inspired by work garments.

"Chanel advocates for pockets
the same way she loyally advocated
for jersey."

(Vogue 1920)

It has been said that no one wears Chanel like Chanel. This photo of Coco taken in 1926, wearing a simple knit suit that complements her androgynous figure, is the proof. The suit's elegant femininity is accented with costume jewelry and pearls.

Right: In the 1920s, when Coco bought a dark blue Rolls Royce with a custom black leather interior, she launched the trend of dark-colored cars. Here she is seen in Biarritz in 1928.

"When I find a color darker than black, I'll wear it. But until then, I'm wearing black!"

In line with her conviction that "elegance signifies condensing everything into the most expensive, chic, refined poverty," she began work on her most inventive project, the creation of a simple black dress suitable for every occasion, a sheath in *crêpe de Chine* that would become a must in every woman's wardrobe. Her *petite robe noire* or little black dress became a symbol of the decade. It was a revisited version of the modest black dress with white cuffs and collar worn by shop assistants and clerks, but it was also tangible confirmation of the obstinate female demand for democratization that was sweeping society, with Coco as its spokesperson.

The quintessence of Parisian chic, it was a simple model that did away with the constraints of bustiers and corsets, made for the casual woman who wanted to dress by herself and undress herself in the blink of an eye.

Once again, inspiration came from Gabrielle's childhood and the memory of the simple habits worn by the nuns of the Aubazine Abbey. Her seemingly austere little black dress proved to have a mysterious sensuality, thanks to her skillful tailoring of plunging backs and asymmetric hemlines. *Vogue* compared it to Ford's Model T, "something the world could not have done without."

The petite robe noire *marked a turning point in fashion. Here, Coco lights up her little black dress with a casual mixture of real jewels and fake stones to create a sensational combination.*

Coco's business in Paris was booming, so she could finally have the sumptuous residence she had always wanted. She left the villa in Garches and rented an apartment in Count Pillet-Will's hotel at 29 Faubourg-Saint-Honoré in the heart of Paris. Her home initially occupied the ground floor but soon expanded to include the floor above as well. The 18th-century palazzo had very high ceilings and a series of enormous rooms, illuminated by French doors that overlooked the gardens where centuries-old horse chestnut, linden, and plane trees were reflected in the pool. She decided she would play with contrasts to furnish the apartment, rather than the classical style that baroque architecture traditionally called for. The first object she brought into her new house was a Russian icon that Stravinsky had given her as a thank-you for her hospitality at Bel Respiro. The composer was hopelessly in love with her, but she never returned his love. Coco spared no expense. She scandalized her friends with purchases such as the Savonnerie rug she bought for one hundred thousand francs, the Louis XV white chairs, the velvet Regency sofa, and the enormous grand piano that would become the focal point of her legendary musical soirees. For years, Coco hosted the era's most important cultural figures, from Cocteau to Colette, but especially Picasso, for whom she kept his own private room because he hated to sleep alone in his house in Rue La Boétie. Reminiscing about the apartment, Coco recalled that there were "plush carpets everywhere, 'colorado claro' in colour, with silky tints, like good cigars, woven to my specification and brown velvet curtains with gold braiding that looked like coronets girdled in silk, from Winston's. I never discussed prices." Her rooms were filled with her beloved Coromandel screens and large mirrors that multiplied lights and perspectives; huge vases of white flowers filled the air with their fragrance.

One of the many artists that were drawn to the house in Rue Faubourg-Saint-Honoré by Coco was the surrealist poet Pierre Reverdy. He was gloomy and provincial and was six years Coco's junior. A friend of Modigliani's, he lived between Montmartre and Montparnasse; but contrary to what one would expect, he was not fond of the *bohémien* lifestyle. In fact, though he despised money, he adored luxury. Coco was enchanted by his air of doomed poet; and the fact that he had a wife, Henriette, did not hinder the birth of a romantic liaison, perhaps not quite love, but a feeling that would last until his death. His feelings for her were evident in the dedications he wrote in each of his collections of poems. In one such collection, he wrote "Dear and admirable Coco. Since you give me the joy of liking something about these poems, I give you this book and hope that it serves you as a soft and gentle bedside light"; and, in another, "To my very great and dear Coco, with all my heart until it beats its last."

She considered him the greatest poet in the world and secretly bought all of his manuscripts and entrusted them to publishers so that they could be printed, at her expense. She also deposited a substantial amount of money in his account every month, letting him believe that the money came from royalties on the sales of his poetry collections. Their names were forever linked by an enduring affection and support that remained unchanged, even when he retreated to Solesmes to end his days in a monastic solitude, with "no distraction from God, for as long as He sees fit, in the sun and under the grey sky."

Coco found herself caught up in the whirl of new friendships. Together with Misia Sert, Coco became an assiduous *habitué* of the trendiest Parisian cabaret of the moment, *Le Bœuf sur le Toit*, where the artists of Montparnasse gathered and where she could show off her latest creations. The place was a great success. Behind its lacquered door was a world that evoked the sensational atmosphere of the Ballets Russes and of surrealism with Picabia's painting *L'œil cacodylate* at the center of the scene. Maurice Chevalier and Tristan Tzara could be found seated at the tables, and young Man Ray was paid to be the official photographer. "Pullovers and espadrilles mingled with tulle dresses, without the least discomfort," observed Jean Cocteau, the avant-garde writer, playwright, and poet who captured Coco's attention immediately.

A portrait of the poet Pierre Reverdy. Together with avant-garde artists, he was a central character in Paris's high society and had a close relationship with Coco that lasted a lifetime.

Another habitué was Sergei Diaghilev, a theater impresario whom Coco had met in Venice on her first trip there with Misia. They certainly could not have been called friends, but they were kindred spirits. Stravinsky wrote: "Diaghilev was much better at intuiting the potential for success than he was at judging music. He understood the importance of novelty and he made it work to his advantage." Few could understand him better than Coco; so when he confessed that he was devastated because he had no funds to produce the new version of *The Rite of Spring*, Coco showed her faith in him by loaning him the exorbitant sum of 300,000 francs, on the condition that no one could know where the money had come from. Nevertheless, word got out quickly and she was soon seen as a sponsor and generous supporter of the arts.

Despite the clamorous social effects it had, the gesture was not a calculated one for Coco. She loved dance, as movement and as a metaphor for freedom, and she was struck by the brilliant esthetics of the Ballets Russes and the choreographies of Nijinsky, where music, dance, and visual arts combined to make ballet a complete art. Her interest in dance led to her great friendship with the Ukrainian ballet dancer Serge Lifar, a star of the Opera with a feline-like charm. They posed for a number of photos together, often dressed alike in baggy, masculine pants that no one wore more gracefully than Coco. With his encouragement, she took a few dance lessons from the likes of the star, Isadora Duncan, but it was the theater that paved the way for her collaboration with some of the greatest artists and choreographers of her time. In 1922, when Cocteau decided to stage his adaptation of *Antigone*, with sets designed by Picasso, he asked Coco to design the costumes for the production. He explained to journalists that "she is the greatest stylist of our times and I really can't imagine Oedipus's daughters being badly dressed."

She accepted the challenge and created draped capes in dark jersey, in addition to a series of necklaces in metal and artificial stones, her first collection of costume jewelry. Man Ray photographed the actress Genica Atanasiou in her role as Antigone, with short hair and a face made up in white. She was sensational in her dark wool cape that appeared as archaic as Picasso's masks on the backdrop. Critics were disoriented and refrained from writing anything at all in the theater magazines; but in its February 1923 edition, *Vogue Paris* praised the originality of Chanel's creations: "The neutral colored wool costumes appeared to be actual antique garments, rediscovered centuries later. It's a beautiful reconstruction, in which archaism is brightened by intelligence."

The dancer Serge Lifar. A friend of Coco's, he joined Sergei Diaghilev's dance company, the Ballets Russes. Coco designed a variety of spectacular costumes for the company between 1922 and 1939.

Coco's talent as a costume designer led to other work with Cocteau, including on the famous *Le Train Bleu*, produced by Diaghilev. The costumes signed Chanel were so original that they ended up in the collections of the Victoria and Albert Museum. The ballet was inspired by the express train that connected Paris to the Côte d'Azur at the time. The extremely luxurious train, with its mahogany-paneled compartments, inlay work by René Prou, and Lalique accessories, transported young, athletic passengers to the Riviera. Against an extraordinary backdrop by Picasso, Coco's costumes were her vision of a relaxed but daring style and reflected the same idea of comfort and freedom of movement that she used in her fashion designs. With her Deauville past in mind, she chose jersey to create bathing suits and golf attire as well as tennis outfits that evoked the style of Suzanne Lenglen, the popular French champion who reigned at Wimbledon.

Le Train Bleu opened for the first time on June 13, 1924 at the Théâtre des Champs-Élysées, where it was an enormous success. In the theater to applaud the performance were some of Chanel's best clients, including the Rothschild family, together with Russian aristocrats who had fled the Revolution, and members of the Spanish nobility who were clients of the maison in Biarritz.

A scene from the 1924 ballet Le Train Bleu, *produced by Diaghilev with some of the best artists of the time. The scenario was written by Cocteau, the curtain was painted by Picasso, and the costumes were designed by Chanel.*

Coco was gratified by her work and began salvaging her love life. There was never a lack of admirers and wooers, some of them famous, but she never married. Nor was she able to have the child she had so desired during her great love affair with Boy. She was just over forty when the shadows of her solitude were lifted. It was 1924 when she met Hugh Richard Arthur Grosvenor, duke of Westminster. Bendor, as everyone called him, was fascinating and rich, not to mention married. She was introduced to him during a dinner on his yacht, the four-masted, 220-foot-long *Flying Cloud*, a luxurious, Queen Mary-style schooner, which was docked in the harbor of Monte Carlo. Not knowing how to swim, she was bored to death, so she spent her days studying the uniforms of the forty-man crew, fascinated by the meticulous lines of their blue and white uniforms and by the shape of their hats, which she immediately re-elaborated to add to the collection she was preparing. The duke was dazzled by this young French woman. She was beautiful and independent and had made her way in life without any help from anyone. She gave no importance to his title or his wealth, unlike the other women who surrounded him. He courted her assiduously for six months, smothering her with attention and with expensive gifts that she repaid with equally costly gifts, just to prove that she was not for sale. She showed indifference even when he sent her a basket of vegetables, cultivated in an English greenhouse and sent to her across the English Channel on the day they were harvested, with a raw emerald as big as a strawberry hidden at the bottom.

One of the rare photos of Coco Chanel together with the duke of Westminster, taken at the Grand National steeplechase in March 1925.

Bendor rolled out a golden carpet at Coco's feet, but she was hesitant, undecided if she should barter those luxuries with the absolute freedom she had enjoyed. After all, it would certainly not be flowers and jewels that would conquer a woman who carried her freedom like a banner and who did not intend to play the role of mistress with a married man. All the tabloids jumped on the news, but the magazine *Star* was the first to report that "much is being said about a duke whose marital spats are creating a stir. Those in the know confirm that the new duchess of Westminster will be a French woman, a beautiful brilliant woman who controls the destiny of a great Parisian fashion house." Before anything else could happen, public opinion had already decided that they were a sensational couple, and when he filed for divorce, Coco surrendered to the fact that theirs would be the most glamorous relationship of the day. Their life as a couple was a fairy tale spent between hunts and cruises, surrounded by important guests like Winston Churchill, even though it was lived in strictly separate homes, as etiquette dictated at the time. The future prime minister was highly impressed by Coco, whom he judged to be at least as clever and determined as he was and, as kindred spirits, they would always be bound by their sincere friendship. Churchill's admiration for Coco was evident in the letter he wrote to his wife Clementine: "The famous Coco Chanel arrived and I took a great fancy to her, a most capable and agreeable woman—much the strongest personality Benny has yet been up against. She hunted vigorously all day, motored to Paris after dinner, and is today engaged in passing and improving dresses on endless streams of mannequins." At the side of the man considered the richest in all of England, the shy Aubazine orphan found retribution in the regal lifestyle he showed her. She admitted "I was treated to a level of luxury that no one will ever know," and in fact the idea of becoming duchess began to take hold in her mind. After the duke's divorce from his second wife was finalized, the couple spent long periods at Eaton Hill, the estate outside Chester where the duke had grown up under the guidance of his grandfather, surrounded by halls full of portraits of his ancestors and paintings of racehorses. Coco loved the endless, rugged countryside; it reminded her of her younger years, spent at the estate of Étienne Balsan, and her relationship with Bendor was idyllic. In love with the duke and in love with the horses, she gladly accompanied him to the Grand National annual steeplechase in Liverpool, on a special train he rented every year for his invited guests. It was at this old English event that one of the rare photographs of them alone together was taken; Coco was swaddled in soft furs and white net stockings that only she could pull off with such style. She put her mind to learning English with the help of the duke's secretary and, to show his appreciation for her effort and to ease the tension that being far from her work was causing, the duke recreated a corner of her Rue Cambon atelier in the family palace that included workrooms staffed with personnel brought from France.

With Winston Churchill and his son Randolph during a hunt at Dieppe, in 1928. When the future prime minister of the United Kingdom and Coco Chanel were introduced by the duke of Westminster, they immediately felt an instinctive connection.

"An interior is the natural projection of one's soul, and Balzac was right in giving it the same importance as to dress." This was what Coco had in mind in 1927, when she renovated her second-floor showroom in the Rue Cambon, giving it a sensational modern feel that was both simple and refined, just like she was. She made the walls disappear, knocking them down when she could or hiding them behind panels of mirrors that created the illusion of infinite space, like a kaleidoscope. She covered the floors with beige carpeting and installed pendant dome fixtures that illuminated everything with diffused light. Placed prominently in the center of the showroom was a staircase with a wrought-iron handrail, which would become legendary, where Coco crouched, hidden from the audience, leaning forward with her arms wrapped around her knees, to watch her latest creations walk down the runway and observe the reactions from her clients.

The showroom in Rue Cambon 31 photographed by Doisneau. It was Mademoiselle's domain and had infinity mirrors that made it appear even more spacious. Standing out in the middle is the legendary staircase that connected the atelier to the showroom.

Coco Chanel in her English period, wearing a striped vest, inspired by those used by the duke's servants, and a hat reminiscent of the ones used by yacht crews. Behind her is one of the precious Coromandel screens from her collection. "I've always loved Chinese screens, and when I went into a shop and saw a Coromandel for the first time, I almost fainted from the joy. The screens were the first interior design elements I bought," she recalled.

At the same time, Chanel fashion was evolving, with new inspiration coming from Coco's everyday life. Her relationship with the duke may have run its course, but the English tailoring style would always be a part of her collections. Life on board the *Flying Cloud* inspired the striped sailor-style top with gold buttons and the sailor cap, decorated with a molten glass pin, to wear tilted down to the brow. Navy blue became part of the Chanel color palette. A version of the striped vests used by the duke's servants, creatively adapted to her models' chests, also became part of the new collection. The enjoyment she found in stealing comfortable, sporty clothing from the wardrobes of gentlemen when she went on hunts with her friend Misia Sirt was her inspiration to introduce the use of tweed into her collections. She took that most masculine of fabrics and transformed it into soft feminine jackets, adorned with gold buttons. She was the first to use tweed in *haute couture*, just as she had been the first to use jersey. The fabric arrived from Scotland, where weavers in the area of the River Tweed had been working with wool since the middle ages, producing irregularly woven cloth that was pleasantly coarse to the touch. The fabrics produced exclusively for Chanel on the 19th-century looms at Linton were lighter and finer than traditional tweeds, and they were hand-dyed in pastel shades that had never been used for tweed in England. "I arranged for woolens to be washed less, so that they kept their softness," explained Coco years later, when she chose the precious fabric to launch her famous collarless jacket, cut from tweed created by Linton exclusively for her, in one-of-a-kind patterns and colors.

A portrait published in the American magazine Vanity Fair *in 1931. At the time, Chanel's success was soaring in the United States and a large part of her wealthy clients was from overseas.*

Her ties to England were evident in other instances as well. In the summer of 1927, her creations made landfall in London with the opening of her new shop in Mayfair. There, she presented a collection created exclusively for the English market that included "gowns for debutantes at court and refined afternoon dresses for Ascot, worn by English models who walked down the runway, as graceful and lissome as lilies," as reported by *Vogue*. Shortly afterward, when the War Service Legion asked the Duke of Windsor for financial assistance, he persuaded Coco to organize a fashion-show benefit, with 130 creations made exclusively from English fabric and modeled for the event by young ladies from London's high society. The *Daily Mail* enthusiastically described the initiative, attended by hundreds of women who were accompanied by their own seamstresses because Coco had given authorization to copy the designs, since they would not be put into production. What initially appeared to be an economic loss proved to be just one more stroke of genius. Photos of the guests, wearing their copies of the original designs, were seen all around the world, including on the pages of the American *Harper's Bazaar*, giving the Chanel brand a sensational return in terms of image, even on the other side of the ocean.

A short time later, Coco presented a collection of light, ethereal evening gowns that conquered the American clientele and brought the echo of her fame to the ears of Sam Goldwyn as well. The legendary movie producer from Metro-Goldwyn-Mayer made her the most extraordinary proposal she had ever received: he would pay her a million dollars to travel to Hollywood twice a year to dress the Hollywood stars of his movies in Chanel creations, on stage and in real life. She was hesitant. After all, she already had all the money she needed, and the richest women in America were already her clients. But when the French fashion industry was hit by the crisis that ensued after the 1929 Wall Street crash, she was forced to cut the prices of her pieces in half and reduce her personnel. So when Goldwyn insisted with his proposal, she finally gave in and, ignoring her infallible intuition, she threw herself into a venture that would turn out to be a failure. Yet, when she arrived in New York in April 1931, everything seemed to be fine. She brought her friend Misia Sert with her from Paris, along with three assistants, two models, three servants, fifteen trunks, and thirty-five suitcases. The small army that boarded the special train headed to Los Angeles with her included a group of journalists that reported on the event. Goldwyn went all out to welcome Mademoiselle in style. The entire train was repainted beige, Coco's color of choice, and, to alleviate the boredom, rivers of champagne flowed during the five-thousand-kilometer trip. A number of Hollywood stars were lined up on the platform to greet the train when it arrived, including Greta Garbo with an armful of orchids. Headlines read: "Two queens meet." There was an immediate connection between the two, just as there was with Marlene Dietrich, who won Coco over with an androgynous style so similar to her own. With a cigarette dangling from her lips and a preference for trousers, Dietrich, who Cocteau said had "a name that starts with a caress and ends with a whip," had a profile that resembled Coco's, and she would always remain faithful to the Rue Cambon style.

Over the following few weeks, Coco met an array of actors and directors, but she was more interested in the decorators and costume designers, even knowing that her Parisian experience with the Ballets Russes and Cocteau's production were nothing compared to the demands of Hollywood sets. From the artisans of the movie world, she learned what was photogenic—a lesson that, wittingly or unwittingly, she would always take into consideration for her creations as well as for her own image. When she got back to Paris, her first job was with Gloria Swanson for the movie *Tonight or Never*, a romantic comedy about an opera star. At the time, the actress was expecting a child with the playboy Michael Farmer, a scandal that had to be kept a secret since the two were not married. In her autobiography, *Swanson on Swanson*, she narrated her embarrassment when, at the meeting with Coco at the atelier in Rue Cambon, she was forced to hide the cause of her sudden weight gain. She described Chanel as "small and impetuous, and as usual, with her hat on during our fitting. She gave me a furious look when she saw I was struggling to fit into the black satin floor length dress, a masterpiece she had measured me for six weeks earlier."

The movie was a success, but it took Coco only a few weeks and even fewer movies to understand that the venture was not working. Movies could never do justice to her quiet colors and understated elegance, and journalists agreed with her, giving her effort just a few lines of coverage in the press. Even the stars seemed to have trouble appreciating French fashion. For them, it was too removed from the sparkle and glamour of Hollywood parties, where the primary goal was to get as much attention as possible.

The New Yorker anticipated the imminent breakup: "The movie gave Gloria the chance to show off an array of costumes. They were designed by Chanel, the famous Parisian whose recent visit to Hollywood caused such a stir. But it doesn't look like she wants to come back to our city of lights and knowledge any time soon, since the movie tycoons made it clear that her costumes weren't sensational enough. The fact is, Chanel makes a lady look like a lady but Hollywood wants a lady to look like two ladies."

Gloria Swanson wearing one of the costumes Chanel designed for the 1931 movie Tonight or Never.

Coco with the actress Ina Claire, star of the 1932 Hollywood movie The Greeks Had a Word for Them, *for which Coco designed the costumes.*

Her American adventure would have turned out to be a fiasco had it not been for Coco's extraordinary business sense. She took advantage of the opportunity to form solid connections with the country's world of high fashion and extend her influence. She was warmly welcomed by two female editors: the editor of *Vogue*, Margaret Case; and the editor of *Harper's Bazaar*, Carmel Snow. Both had emigrated from Russia and were well aware of the ties she had formed with their compatriots, to whom she entrusted primary roles in her Parisian atelier, not to mention her rapport with Diaghilev and the Ballets Russes. As she was out walking around the streets of New York, Coco made another discovery: she sensed that the future of *prêt-à-porter* was under the skyscrapers of Fifth Avenue. She visited the downtown department stores and saw that in the windows of Macy's and Bloomingdales there were copies of her designs, made from inferior quality materials but with her unmistakable style. She was not at all bothered and saw no problem with the display. Quite the contrary, she felt it proved the value of her creations. After all, in her opinion, "fashion that doesn't reach the streets isn't fashion." New

challenges were waiting when she got back to Paris. Her relationship with the duke had been faltering for some time. He smothered her with attention, but he had one terrible defect: his infidelity. It was a terrible insult for a woman as proud as Coco. With bitter clarity, she saw herself becoming once again prisoner of a disheartening, deceitful relationship, as she had been so many years before with Boy. Hoping to be forgiven, Bendor gave her expensive gifts, such as the emerald that she threw into the sea when they were on a cruise, a gesture worthy of young Cleopatra who dissolved Caesar's pearls in vinegar. When the duke announced that he wanted a child, Coco, who was nearing fifty, knew that her hopes of becoming a mother were few and that an end to their story was inevitable. So she pushed him into the arms of the baroness Loelia Mary Ponsonby, who became his third wife but was never able to give him the heir he so badly wanted. As proud as ever, when someone asked why she had not married the duke, Coco purportedly answered with one of her shocking statements: "There have been several duchesses of Westminster but there is only one Chanel!"

She was not alone for long. She accepted the attentions of Paul Iribarnegaray, a talented decorator of Basque origins. He was a friend of artists and actors, including Cocteau, who introduced them. Iribe, as he was nicknamed, was brilliant and ambitious, robust but elegant with thick wavy hair and intense eyes behind gold-rimmed glasses. A ladies' man, he had been married to the actress Jeanne Dirys, who had graced the cover of *Comœdia Illustré* in 1911, wearing one of Chanel's hats, and at the time had a new American wife with a sizable fortune that was quickly running out. According to gossip, he was hiding a murky past as a gigolo to wealthy women who had maintained him in a life of luxury. When they met, around 1930, Coco was at the peak of her glory, still beautiful and immensely wealthy. They discovered that they had both been born in the same year and that they shared an infinity of interests. He had worked for the stylist Paul Poiret for years, he collaborated with *Vogue*, his drawings were magnificent, and he had invented the famous *Arpège* perfume bottle, the *boule noire*, with the image of a woman with a turban reaching down for a little girl that symbolized Jeanne Lanvin's love for her daughter Marie-Blanche.

A portrait of Iribe, pseudonym of Paul Iribarnegaray, a talented illustrator and decorator who met Coco Chanel in 1930. Their intense love affair and creative partnership had lasted only five years when it was abruptly interrupted by his death in 1935.

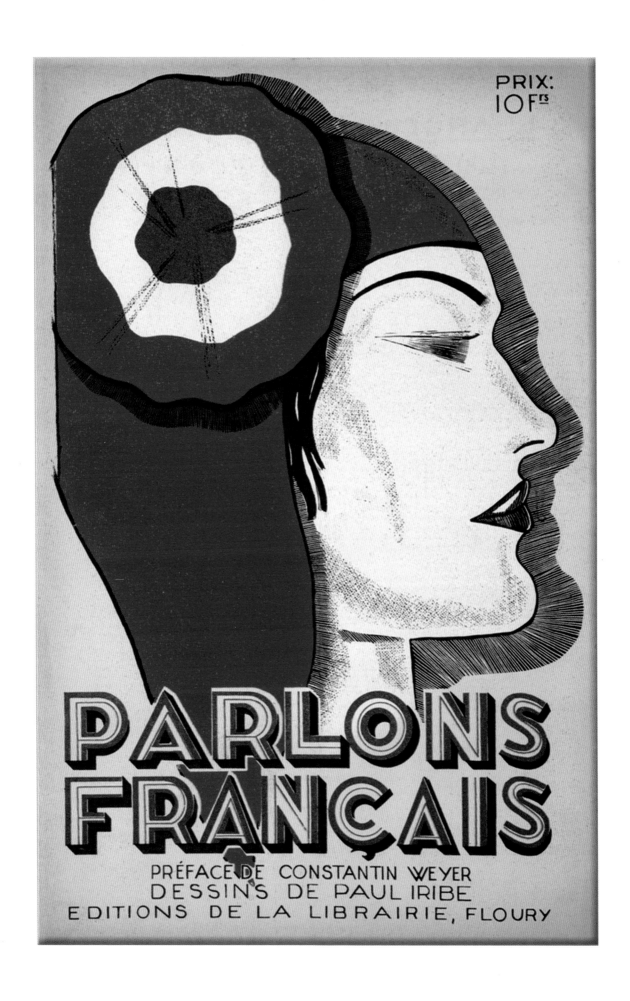

Iribe loved luxury, and he moved with nonchalance in what would now be defined as the world of design, creating crystal bottles for Lalique and selling originally styled designer furniture. His tiny boutique in Faubourg-Saint-Honoré was a treasure chest of Art Deco, where he displayed impeccable combinations of *bergère* armchairs with carved spirals, gilded wood furniture, and daring ebony sculptures from Madagascar, where he was said to have spent part of his mysterious childhood.

Coco was in love again. She shared Iribe's tastes and style, and soon he became not just her lover but her most important associate as well. He was strong-willed and unscrupulous, capable of persuading a woman as determined and intransigent as Coco to entrust him with the management of the shield that guaranteed her financial independence, the Société des Parfums, which was generating most of her earnings, thanks to the everlasting success of Chanel N° 5. In exchange, he immortalized her unmistakable face, transforming it into a portrait of Marianne, the personification of the French Republic, with forceful features colored in black, red, and blue. The image was to be published in the *Le Témoin* magazine where Iribe worked as editor, columnist, and primary illustrator.

This lithograph by Iribe, published in the periodical Le Témoin *in July 1934, hides a tribute to his lover: the facial features of Marianne, the symbol of France, resemble those of Coco.*

Wrapped up in an intense relationship that combined affection, interests, and creativity, they often worked as a duet, making costume jewelry, Coco's new passion. "What counts isn't the carats, it's the illusion," she explained. In fact, Chanel is credited with inventing *bijoux de couture*, or fashion jewelry, original creations intended to complete stylists' high-fashion looks. She loved to combine her simple designs with flashy, affordable accessories made of crystals, semi-precious stones, faux pearls, and metal that could be worn every day. For her own wear, she preferred genuine jewels. In a photo taken in Paris in 1936 by Boris Lipnitzki, Coco is wearing her ever-present six strands of pearls. She was superstitious and considered them a good luck charm, to be worn knotted over her suits or shirts, whether it was day or night. Her favorites were the excessively long *sautoirs* of faux pearls that hung down to her waist, which she used to make herself appear taller and to brighten her little black dresses. Once again, her sources of inspiration were both assorted and unexpected. She dipped into medieval and byzantine art to create the orthodox-style crosses adorned with colored stones that were as striking as the stain-glassed windows that told stories of saints and filled the churches of the middle ages with light. Her memories of Aubazine can be seen in her costume jewelry as well: the geometric decorations of the windows where she first had glimpsed the interlocking Cs that would become her trademark and the Maltese cross made of a mosaic of river stones on the floor that had been walked on by so many young girls.

On the facing page and on those that follow are the photos from the famous series shot by Boris Lipnitzki in Paris in 1936. Coco Chanel was already a style icon, posing with the confidence of a star. Standing out on a simple black sweater, her real jewels and costume jewelry intertwine with her pearls. She is also wearing clip earrings that she designed with a half mabé pearl surrounded by diamond petals.

With the duke Fulco di Verdura in 1937. Together they created the iconic bangle, the cream-colored enamel cuff bracelet decorated with a Maltese cross made of colored gems.

Soon Chanel began to produce long necklaces made of glass beads, and enamel bracelets to wear as a contrast with her pure minimalist-style dresses, or by day with a simple pullover. She was a woman of a thousand intuitions; to collaborate with her in this new sector, she chose two friends, the count Étienne de Beaumont and the duke Fulco di Verdura, both of whom were men of the world with impeccable taste and the ability to guarantee widespread visibility for her latest creations. Beaumont, an antiques collector, designed a Chanel classic that is still in production—a pendant encrusted with stones and accompanied by long gold chains. Coco met the duke, a Sicilian jeweler and cousin of the writer Tomasi di Lampedusa, at a ball in Venice organized by Cole Porter. He was the inventor of her very famous bangle, the white enamel cuff bracelet decorated with the Maltese cross that has been one of the brand's best sellers since 1937. A short time later, she commissioned François Hugo, a descendant of the poet and the operations manager at the Chanel jersey factories, to create pins, clips, and sets of costume jewelry that were flashy but affordable. When she placed them on the basic lines of her dresses, she was clearly breaking with tradition and proposing to democratize not only the dress but its accessories as well. The creations were luxurious, almost opulent, because Coco loved the simplicity of the dress, but she loved enriching it with contrasting, whimsical accessories just as much. "Jewelry from jewelry shops bores me," she explained. She did nothing to hide her distaste for overly simple settings and traditional jewels, which she found mundane. "You might as well wear a check around your neck," she declared, adding "For that matter, the most beautiful jewelry makes me think of wrinkles, loose skin of wealthy widows,

At work in 1937, with the glasses she was rarely seen wearing in photos, even though she always kept them close at hand, together with her cigarettes, in the comfortable pockets of her suits.

bony fingers, death and last wills and testaments." And yet she owned a lot of splendid jewels, many of which were gifts from past lovers, like Dmitri and the duke of Westminster, but many that she bought for herself, once she finally had the means to satisfy a whim for stones of immeasurable value. Some were so big and so precious that no one would have imagined they were real when she showed them off, nonchalantly mixed with pieces of costume jewelry over plain sweaters, to exalt their beautiful essentiality. Among her favorites was an inexpensive ring with a colored crystal ringed in gold. Whether it was on her left pinky finger or on a chain, hidden under her blouse, she never took it off. It was said that she had received it when she was twenty and just starting out as a clerk in Moulins. It was a gift from a stranger who predicted that her future would be full of money and men.

In 1932, she surprised everyone with a Hollywood-worthy staging of her first and only high-jewelry collection, certainly with the help of Iribe. The move appeared to be contrary to all of her convictions, but she justified it in an interview with the Parisian newspaper *L'Intrasigeant*, saying "In my profession, there are many instruments that are legitimate as long as they are used only for fashion in the truest sense of the word. What initially impelled me to create costume jewelry was its lack of arrogance in an era in which ostentation was too easily available, an aspect that fades in a period of economic crisis, when an instinctive need for authenticity in all things leads us to consider the value of silly trinkets as only what they are actually worth." On November 7, elegant members of Paris's high society lined up in Faubourg-Saint-Honoré to see the exhibit of jewels created by Chanel, entitled *Bijoux de Diamants*. For the occasion, Coco opened the door to her private home, moving all her furniture out of the ground floor to make way for the display cases. She left the apartment a few months later. to move to a new one in the Rue Cambon.

The staging that welcomed guests was stunning. Mirrors reflected the sparkle of the stones, multiplying them to infinity in the penumbra that was favored at the time, created by the soft, indirect light cast by the room's crystal chandeliers. Marble columns held 19th-century polished-wax busts with made-up eyes and bright red lips, which Coco had dug out of the back of her Paris shop, wearing tiaras and pins shaped like stars, leaves, and half-moons. White dominated everything with diamonds as the absolute star of the show. She invented transformable pieces that met with great success, including a necklace with an invisible mechanism that became a hatpin and three bracelets. The highlight of the exhibit was a fringe of diamonds that was to be worn on one's forehead, like a sparkling veil, in combination with the Cometè, a necklace with no clasp that wrapped halfway around the neck in a sinuous cascade of diamonds. None of the jewelry was for sale, unlike the luxurious catalogs with photos taken by Robert Bresson, a young filmmaker with a promising future who later directed the movie *Les Dames du Bois de Boulogne*. Proceeds from catalog sales went to two charitable causes chosen by Coco. As always, immediate earnings were not her goal. Instead, she counted on the great visibility that the initiative would bring; she was not disappointed.

The day after the exhibit, the caricaturist Sem, with his usual biting tone, announced, "Finally, the real has decided to copy the false." Stock in the De Beers diamond company rose by twenty points and the name Chanel was in newspapers all over the world, with over 250 articles dedicated to the event.

One of the mannequins displayed at the exposition Bijoux de Diamants *in 1932. The only collection of precious jewelry designed by Chanel, it was presented at her private apartment in Faubourg-Saint-Honoré.*

Coco Chanel's apartment in the Rue Cambon in Paris, photographed by Cecil Beaton for Vogue.

Soon after, seduced by her passion for accessories and inspired by Iribe, she threw herself into furnishing the new apartment on the second floor of Rue Cambon 31, a large space studied in every detail to impress her guests. It was a treasure chest of curiosities, illuminated by six enormous windows that looked out over the street. The door opened onto an entryway where Coco displayed a pair of precious renaissance statues of two life-sized moors and a monumental 18th-century *bergère* armchair upholstered in white satin, where she was often photographed. The beloved lacquered Coromandel screens that lined the salon were decorated with figures from Chinese culture using a technique dating to the Han dynasty, despite being named for a region in India where they had been stored before being shipped to Europe. The most precious screens were those situated beside her beige suede sofa, where she loved to relax and where she was often immortalized in photos, posed with pillows made of the same quilted leather she would later use to make the first bag with the Chanel name. Her furnishings were characterized by the same freedom she took in her work as a stylist. Coco poured her passionate personality into the rooms and broke with convention to mix antique objects with souvenirs. She claimed that "What counts is that the single elements are beautiful." The objects she displayed on her tables included small, precious knickknacks, jewelry boxes, crystal balls, Hindu statues, and a golden hand sculpted for her by Alberto Giacometti, in addition to precious *vermeil* boxes, red on the outside and gold on the inside,

with the Westminster crest. The duke had given them to her during their love affair to prove the elegance of hidden English luxury, repeating to her that "the inside is just as important as the outside." The andirons were the work of the cubist sculptor Jacques Lipchitz. Many objects were branded with the N° 5 or the interlocking Cs, or a G, the first initial of her given name. Illuminated by the crystal chandeliers, gold was reflected on every surface, caressing the bronze deer statues that had belonged to the Marquise Casati with soft light. In addition to a miniature zoo full of real and imaginary creatures of glass and porcelain, often in couples, she collected dozens of lions, her zodiac sign. They came from every era and were made of all kinds of material. The fact that she believed them to be actual good-luck charms was proof of her superstitious side. The Russian icon Stravinsky gave her hung next to ethnic masks and the only two paintings in her home, one by Dalí and the other by Fautrier. Books, on the other hand, were abundant. Black- and beige-bound editions of the works of Shakespeare, Voltaire, Byron, and Brontë sat alongside books written by those friends who had taught her to love reading, such as Reverdy and Cocteau, as well as a consumed copy of the Sanskrit poem *Bhagavad Gita* that she had received from Boy, with his annotations. An avid reader, she considered books her "best friends," not objects to put on display, so much so that she entrusted the management of her personal library to the writer Maurice Sachs, who added to it over the years, according to Mademoiselle's evolving tastes.

To work on her creations, she retired to
her studio (the door still has a sign that says
"Mademoiselle Privé"), where her screens hung
like panels applied to the walls like wainscoting.
The apartment had a bathroom with a dressing
table full of crystal candelabras, *vermeil* boxes,
and immaculate towels, as well as a kitchen,
since Coco loved to dine in at Rue Cambon,
where she was never alone at the table. She
used the Louis XIII table that dominated the
dining room to receive clients and friends,
including Elizabeth Taylor and Pablo Picasso,
as well as members of her staff, models, and
tailors. The house in the Rue Cambon had
everything except a bed. She had purchased it as
an atelier, without a permit to transform it into
a residence; and in fact, it served as a drawing
room for her private meetings, connected to the
atelier via the famous mirrored staircase. She
slept in her suite on the top floor of the Hotel
Ritz for 34 years, leaving to go back to work
every day in the late morning. The suite was
conveniently connected to the Rue Cambon by
a secret passageway through the kitchen that
allowed her to go from her suite to the back
door of the hotel in the Place Vendôme, right
in front of the entrance to the atelier, without
being seen.

*Left: Coco, surrounded by books and animal knickknacks in the
living room of her apartment in the Rue Cambon.*

*Top: The entrance to her private studio, which was concealed
behind a door marked "Mademoiselle Privé."*

Top: Coco, lying in her bed in Villa La Pausa, photographed by Roger Schall in 1938. One of her favorite symbols, a five-point star, stands out on the headboard. The star was a reminder of the decorations at the orphanage in Aubazine, where she spent her childhood. It became a recurring theme in her jewelry.

Right: She was impeccable even when she went to bed in her custom-made, masculine pajamas in cream-colored or black satin. The photo was taken in her suite at the Hotel Pierre in New York in 1931.

Coco Chanel in her suite at the Hotel Ritz in the Place Vendôme in Paris. Every evening for 34 years, she came home to her suite after a day's work in the Rue Cambon.

Coco spent the summer at the Villa La Pausa, on the French Riviera, with Iribe. One of the couple's guests, the writer Paul Morand, described the carefree life they lived there: "Yesterday I went to dinner at Chanel's. She was so dainty in her little white barman's jacket and when we had finished eating, Coco, Iribe and Constant Say started a game of pelota."

She loved spending her days outdoors, with the cicadas singing in the background, in this home that had been created just for her. She had first had the idea of the villa in 1929 while she was spending her time on the Riviera with the duke of Westminster.

She had seen a piece of land overlooking the sea at Roquebrune-Cap-Martin that was part of the Grimaldi family's hunting grounds, and it was on these two hectares, planted with olive trees and wild orange trees with an extraordinary view of the Italian coast on the horizon, that she decided to build the Mediterranean villa of her dreams. She enlisted the architect Robert Streitz to design three buildings, arranged around an external patio with columns, that would become one big home. In addition to the main house, there were two guest houses in the olive grove where she offered hospitality to her visitors, the most assiduous of whom was Winston Churchill, who wrote his *History of the English Speaking People* during his stays in the villa. When she saw the preliminary drawings, she asked Streitz to add a large staircase to the entrance, identical to the one in Aubazine, the abbey-transformed-into-orphanage where she had spent her adolescence. For the roof, she demanded 20,000 original tiles, pillaged from ancient Provencal houses, that cost their weight in gold. On the inside, the style was grandiose but austere, characterized by large airy rooms painted white and softened by brown and beige rugs, comfortable rustic furnishings, Spanish wrought-iron lights hanging from the ceiling, and a few precious renaissance pieces given to her by the duke at the time of their relationship. *Vogue* dedicated an article titled *At home with Chanel* to this jewel nestled in the heart of the Mediterranean. The article portrayed Coco in the unprecedented role of the perfect hostess. She was a master of style in interior design and, once again, she was a forerunner of trends that stylists such as Armani and Ralph Lauren would propose half a century later. During those years, the color of the lavender blooming in the gardens of the villa made it into the Chanel collections, in tulle and chiffon dresses that looked like they had arisen from the spray of the waters on the French Riviera.

It was an explosion of romanticism that marked the end of an era. It was there, in the Villa La Pausa, that the last chapter of the love story between Coco and Iribe played out. Their extraordinary artistic affinity might have assured Coco a long, happy life at this man's side if a heart attack had not struck him down suddenly on September 21, 1935, as she was holding him in her arms after a game of tennis, in the home that both of them loved so much. When night fell, she was alone again.

The Return of the Queen

Chanel's second life began when she was seventy. To everyone's surprise, she came back, triumphant, once again dictating the rules of simple, timeless elegance, challenging the world of haute couture *with her quilted bag, her two-toned pump, and a knit suit that even Jackie Kennedy wore.*

In 1936, the Chanel brand was at the height of its fame. The atelier employed almost 4,000 people and sold 28,000 extremely expensive articles every year, throughout the world. Coco was devastated by the death of Iribe and threw herself into her work. Years later, she would reveal to Raymond Massaro, her trustworthy shoe supplier who had just been widowed, her secret for not sinking into despair: "There's one thing you must never forget, Raymond. If one day you're alone and full of pain, without anyone or anything, there is always a friend whose door you can knock on: your work." In October, the atelier in the Rue Cambon was buzzing with the preparations for the spring collection, filled with bolts of fabric and wall mirrors. Colette described the work that was going on: "Mademoiselle is busy carving a serene beautiful blond and gold angel that, at times, teeters in the hands of its creator. Chanel works with all ten fingers, with her nails, with the heels of her hand and her palms, using pins and scissors, directly on the dress. At times she kneels down in front of her creation and hugs it, not to venerate it but to try to keep the tulle from puffing out. Oh, the ardent humility of the body in front of its favorite creation! Chanel was bent forward with her feet folded under her knees, like a washerwoman sitting on the ground to beat her clothes, or like the robust housewives who were forced twenty times a day to kneel as our nuns did."

Coco Chanel in the Rue Cambon atelier, surrounded by her models, all of whom had the same hairstyle as she.

Mademoiselle never stopped talking, giving orders to an army of seamstresses and assistants who were handing her fabrics and black trays full of jewels to pair with the dresses. Around her neck, she wore a piece of packing string with a pair of Nogent scissors, the best in the world. She considered the scissors to be the instrument of her trade, not needles or pins, because she was a tailor who loved to cut and did not love to sew. "I'm an instrument of fate in a necessary cleanup operation," she said. "Is there anything sentimental about the lines of an airplane? No. And I created my collections thinking about airplanes."

The Chanel atelier in London in the 1930s. The model standing next to Coco is Lady Pamela Smith, a socialite who was one of the ambassadors of the Chanel style.

Top: Coco Chanel in 1937. The simple elegance of her style is perfectly reflected in one of her famous phrases: "Some people think luxury is the opposite of poverty. It is not. It is the opposite of vulgarity."

Right: A famous portrait shot by Cecil Beaton in London in 1935, published in Vogue.

The winds of protest were blowing around her, and the wave of strikes that followed the French elections in 1936 did not spare Rue Cambon, where a banner that read "Occupied" hung outside. The atmosphere was tense. Coco was on one side, shocked and angry, demanding the fruits of her tireless work; and her workers were on the other, demanding paid vacation time, even though she had made an apartment in the greenery of Landes available to them and allowed them to spend a few days of vacation there, without losing their pay. As tensions continued to rise, Coco made an unexpected proposal, offering to turn the company over to her employees. Interested only in creating, she would be the director and receive a salary from them. They refused the proposal, but the rift was mended and work could begin again.

The strikes were not her only worry. For the first time in fifteen years, her competition was looming and Chanel had begun to lose ground. It was Elsa Schiaparelli, an Italian born in Rome to an aristocratic family, who competed with her for dominance. After Schiaparelli's divorce from the Count of Kerlor, she moved to Paris where she frequented a group of Dadaists. She began sewing skirts in a studio in the Rue de Seine; but before long she was successful enough to open a shop in the Place Vendôme, right next to Chanel. Her extravagant creations were inspired by the esthetics of surrealism, and to give them an even more eccentric touch she used extremely novel materials such as a transparent plastic called rhodophane, as well as lobster prints for her skirts, shrimp-shaped buttons, and drawer-shaped pockets. Chanel was beside herself with the thought that any woman was willing to wear such circus costumes, but she limited her reaction to a vein of sarcasm and relegated Elsa's creations to the realm of vulgarity when the stylist designed a black dress that had taffeta hands across each breast. The truce held until Schiaparelli openly challenged Chanel, launching a line of perfumes, *Schiap* in 1934 and *Shocking* in 1938. It was war. From that moment on, Coco began to call her competitor "the Italian who sews dresses" and prohibited the mention of Schiaparelli's name in her presence.

The strikes in 1936 affected Chanel along with others. Seamstresses and clerks blocked the personnel entryway and hung up shoe boxes in which to collect contributions.

Two Chanel designs from the 1938 spring/summer collection. For daywear, she proposed a series of two-piece outfits, with her ever-present pockets, that were made of affordable fabrics such as cotton piqué. The clear-cut simplicity of the garments was exalted by the use of black and white. "Simplicity is the keynote of all true elegance," Coco affirmed.

Refusing to give in to her competition, Coco participated in the 1937 World's Fair. The event saw the construction of the new Trocadero and two pavilions, Germany's with its iron cross and the Soviet Union's with its hammer and sickle, one in front of the other, and a space dedicated to *haute couture*. Inside the Pavillon de l'Elegance, in the Club des Oiseaux, Coco, dressed like her models, watched as her creations walked down the runway to thunderous applause. Black and white, her non-colors, dominated the scene. "Women think of all colors except the absence of color. I have said that black has it all. White too. Their beauty is absolute. It is the perfect harmony," she declared. Underneath that apparent simplicity, details became fundamental. According to Chanel, elegance was "sacrifice, weeding out the excess. A hem, a button, a millimeter of cuff or a ruffle; it's a whole philosophy. It means clothes that are well-made and beautiful to the eye."

Always true to her meticulous lines, she never stopped reinventing the day looks that were some of her initial successes; comfortable jersey dresses and tweed suits that combined elegance and practicality and never lost their lines, not even when they were wrinkled. For her eveningwear, on the other hand, she unleashed all of her creativity, preserving the purity of her shapes and an almost obsessive attention to the details. She suggested that women be caterpillars by day and butterflies by night. "There is nothing more comfortable than a caterpillar and nothing more made for love than a butterfly. We need dresses that crawl

On these pages, two of Chanel's eveningwear creations from 1936. In that period, she introduced new fabrics such as tulle, which she mixed with silk and lace to make gowns that evoked the allure of Hollywood movies. She broadened her color palette beyond her usual black and white to include pastels such as powder blue and lilac.

Top: Coco Chanel photographed as a movie star by Horst P. Horst for Vogue in 1937. She is wearing a lavish white lace gown, a headdress with a feather, and emerald and ruby jewelry.

Right: Coco photographed by François Kollar in her suite at the Hotel Ritz. In 1937, this photo was used in the first advertisement for the brand's perfume, Chanel N° 5.

Coco Chanel with the duke, Fulco di Verdura, at a masquerade ball organized by the prince, Jean-Louis de Faucigny-Lucigne, and the baron, Nicolas de Gunzburg, in 1934.

and dresses that fly. Fashion is at once a caterpillar and a butterfly, caterpillar by day, butterfly by night."

Her crowning glories were the gowns she created for costume balls, where she was allowed to revisit the *belle époque* style that she had banished many years earlier and reinvent it with a touch of irony. Ruffles, bare shoulders, and transparent sleeves made Chanel's women of the late 30s into brilliantly hued butterflies, with a color palette that went beyond black and navy blue and dared to embrace colors like pink, pale green, and sometimes even red. For her more formal evening gowns, she was a master at creating diaphanous silhouettes in tulle and muslin. She also used taffeta, silver brocade silk, and gold lamé, precious fabrics that she embellished with sequins and gold ornaments; but even in her most daring combinations, her designs never came even remotely close to the flamboyance of Schiaparelli. The hats that were invariably part of her collections were true to her style, always simple but never insignificant, adorned with ribbon and flat bows and even with camellias, the flower that was Coco's passion. Pieces of her flashy costume jewelry added the final touch to her creations.

In 1939, with the threat of war hanging over Paris, Chanel introduced a new collection that included "gypsy" looks and a number of "tri-color" dresses that were patriotic only inasmuch as their colors evoked those of the French flag. A few weeks later, the invasion of Poland put an end to the optimism of those who had hoped that a new conflict could be avoided.

When World War II broke out, it forced Rue Cambon to a sudden standstill. At 56, Chanel had reached and surpassed all the goals she had set; so with no man at her side to give her energy and motivation, she decided to retire. With Paris drowning in the darkness of war, she declared "this is no time for dresses," and she closed the shutters in Rue Cambon, resigned to living a quiet existence, far from society. The only shop that remained open was the one that sold perfume, while the dozens of gold and red velvet chairs where clients sat to watch her creations walk down the runway were covered with gray drop cloths. Two thousand, five hundred workers were fired, but she remained on good terms with most of them, despite the abrupt termination. They all knew that they would have no problem finding another job: their experience working at Chanel was worth more than any diploma or endorsement.

During the war, when Madame Lucia, one of the head tailors of the atelier, began dressing Coco in a small workshop that she had opened in Rue Royal, Coco went from her role as Lucia's employer to being her most illustrious client. To execute the designs, the hard-to-please Coco called in Madame Ligeour, known as Manon, who had begun working at Chanel as a seamstress when she was only 13. She went on to make

Mademoiselle's private wardrobe for the rest of her life.

They were difficult times for everyone, and what was left of Coco's rapport with her family fell apart as well. Julia and Antoinette, the sisters who had shared her hard life at the Aubazine orphanage, died in uncertain circumstances that were never clarified. Official documents state that the older sister died of tuberculosis in 1915 and the younger of the Spanish flu in 1920, but Coco suspected that they both had taken their own lives. Both had been disillusioned in love, and both had been condemned to a life that was nothing like the one they had dreamed of as children. Obsessed by the idea, Coco would always link the wedding dress she designed for Antoinette to the unhappiness of her marriage; in the end, she convinced herself that wedding dresses in general brought her bad luck. She was the only couturier who banished them from her collections, and for as long as she was the director, not one bride walked the runway in Rue Cambon. As for her brothers, she felt that she had done more than her due, helping them as much as possible and getting nothing in return. She wrote to both of them to inform them that she no longer intended to send the monthly checks they had been receiving for years. The older of the two, Lucien Chanel, had followed in his father's footsteps, working as a street vendor in the market of Clermont until the time when Coco gave him a considerable sum of money. It was enough, in fact, to build himself a home and to make him financially independent. Alphonse, the other brother, had invested his sister's money in a tobacco shop in Valleraugue, in the Gard region. Every month for twenty-five years, Chanel's clerks had diligently sent money orders to both of them; but from that moment on, the brothers were on their own. Coco broke off all ties with them and never saw them again. The only family tie that remained was with André Palasse, the son of her sister Julia, who had been orphaned at a very early age. She continued to look after him, showering him with the love she would have had for the child that destiny had denied her. On a suggestion from Boy, she paid for him to attend an exclusive English boarding school, where he received a gentleman's education, and bought him a dwelling worthy of nobility, the Chateau Peyros.

Coco decided to stay in Paris during the occupation. They were difficult years for a woman like her, who could not bear listlessness and detested idleness. Her friend Jean Marais, whom she nicknamed Jeannot, was sent to the Somme with his company, the 107 aviation. She proclaimed herself his wartime godmother and sent him boxes of scarves, fur-lined gloves, and mufflers. He wrote with sad irony, "We are the only company in the French army dressed entirely in Chanel."

German soldiers occupied Chanel's suite at the Ritz, along with most of the rest of the hotel.

Everything in the rooms was dismantled, but Chanel's trunks had something different about them and Gerhard Gross, the officer who was overseeing the clearance, noticed them.

When the hotel staff informed him that they were the personal effects of Madame Chanel, he ordered that they be transferred to a secure location. He also managed to find a room for the illustrious guest, whose fame continued to guarantee her special treatment; although Coco would no longer be able to throw open her windows onto the Place Vendôme, she was given a small apartment facing the back of the hotel. Today, the three rooms of Suite Chanel are home to some of the opulent screens from Rue Cambon; but when Coco lived there, the furnishings were spare, with mansard ceilings that reminded her of the room she had shared with her Aunt Adrienne when she was a seamstress in Moulins.

It was the lodging of a young girl with a single bed. Books were spread all over; there was a small statue of St. Anthony of Padua, a souvenir from her first trip to Venice with Misia; there were no pictures; and the windows were always half-closed. "My three garrets: one for sleeping, one for talking, and one for washing," as she defined them.

Luckily for her, she still had the apartment in Rue Cambon. She received her old friends there; the ballet dancer Serge Lifar, who lived nearby, visited almost every day, as did Cocteau and Misia Sert. The days were spent reading and listening to music—in fact, Coco had taken up singing again, to everyone's surprise. An incredulous Misia Sert wrote in her diary, "When I got to Coco's, I heard some amazing trills. There were two witches with bright red manes, one sitting at the piano and one standing with her elbows on the instrument and Coco, standing quietly nearby, listening to their reprimands. It was a singing lesson. Incredible! At 54, she presumes that her voice has a future." The relationship between the two friends had always been a mixture of deep affection and the tension caused by the prickly character they both possessed, but it grew stronger when Misia, who had become addicted to morphine, suffered a heart attack and lost her eyesight due to a retinal hemorrhage. Despite their strong bond, Coco always spoke bitingly about her, in much the same way she ironized about the defects of many of her acquaintances. After all, she herself admitted, "I love to criticize. The day I stop criticizing, my life will be over." A few years later, at the end of their tumultuous friendship, Coco paid her the most moving tribute by dressing her for her funeral service before opening the door to their artist friends who had come to pay their respects. Misia looked more beautiful than ever, lying on a bed of white flowers, dressed completely in white with a pale pink ribbon across her chest where Coco had laid a single rose, her last gift to her friend.

Just when it seemed as though she had become bogged down in a sad routine, fate bestowed on her one last great love: the German diplomat Hans Günther von Dincklage. When she fondly called him "Spatz," or sparrow, she may have been alluding to his reputation as a womanizer, glibly "flitting" from one woman to the next; but he was a modern playboy, well introduced in high society as a diplomatic service officer for the Reich. He was tall and athletic, with blue eyes. Of English heritage on his mother's side, he spoke perfect French and, immediately after divorcing his first wife, he began a brilliant diplomatic career that would allow him access to Paris's most important cultural circles. He loved Paris and the high life, so he readily accepted the role that the government assigned him, despite his lack of great affinity for Nazi convictions. He and Coco had already crossed paths in the past, at the mundane events that both of them attended less and less frequently. During a dinner, Coco spoke to him of her worries about her favorite nephew, André Palasse, who had been taken prisoner by the Germans like millions of other Frenchmen. He offered to help; but six months later, he had yet to obtain any results. In the meantime, the bond between the two had become something more than a tender friendship. After all, Coco was nearing sixty and her solitude was becoming harder to bear. It was no surprise when she replied to those who reproached her for her relationship with the German, saying "At the age I was then, if a man honors you with his courtship, do you ask to see his documents?"

Surrounded by her books in the apartment in Rue Cambon. When the atelier was closed during World War II, the only Chanel display window to stay open was the one at the perfume shop.

In this photo from the early 1950s, Coco's essential black-and-white look was accented with a beret with a veil and a cascade of jewelry in which the authentic jewels were indistinguishable from the costume jewelry.

In an effort to resolve the situation with her nephew, Spatz introduced her to Theodore Momm, a brilliant officer who controlled the French textile industries during the occupation. The two had much in common, considering that among Chanel's businesses, there were two factories that had been closed since 1939 but that were of great strategic importance. Momm himself was at the center of an incident regarding Chanel's relationship with politics during the war that is still shrouded in mystery. Obsessed with putting an end to the war, it seems that in November 1943, Coco did everything in her power to persuade her friend Winston Churchill to open secret talks between the English and German governments. After all, Coco thought that the German government knew it had to take into consideration the idea of defeat and the English government might have been tempted to agree to a compromised peace in order to avoid shedding more blood and tears. Momm made an effort to convince the German high command, and after a trip to Berlin, with the help of the SS officer Walter Schellenberg, he obtained the authorization to launch a diplomatic mission that was dubbed *Operation Modellhut*, or model hat, another clue that pointed to Chanel's involvement, given her activity as a milliner. The plan was to arrange a meeting between Coco and Churchill in Madrid, where she would be permitted to go because she was opening a new branch of her fashion house there. Unfortunately, although the prime minister was actually in Madrid, he was ill and could not receive visitors, so she was unable to meet him. No one will ever know if that meeting would have led to a more rapid solution to the conflict, and this sphere of Coco's activities is still a mystery. Nothing certain emerged from the testimonies given, not even that of Schellenberg during his trial at Nuremberg where he was sentenced to six years, the lightest sentence handed down by the court. All the known facts are narrated in a 1995 BBC documentary entitled *Chanel: a Private Life*, and one of the things that is known for certain is that after that, Coco was put under special surveillance and was added to the list of the Intelligence Service, which certified the identity of French citizens who could be trusted. Disappointed that she had been unable to meet with the prime minister, she returned to Paris, her consolation being that, unlike other colleagues, with her production halted and her business shuttered, she had not given one cent to the Germans. The only relief she found during the long months of inactivity was her affair with Spatz, which proceeded without a fuss, far from prying eyes.

A well-kept secret during the war, the relationship suddenly became public domain a few days after the Liberation on September 10, 1944 when Coco was arrested and accused of consorting with the enemy. The influence of powerful friends like the duke of Westminster or perhaps even Churchill himself was the only reason she was released after just a few hours.

The defamation was impossible to bear. Tired and depressed, she fled to Switzerland, where she went from one hotel to another in a self-imposed exile, far from her work and her motherland, in an attempt to get as far away as possible from the past. After a long stay on Lake Geneva, where she had already transferred her assets, she discovered the Engadin Valley. She spent the winter with her friend and associate Étienne de Beaumont in St. Moritz, where she learned to ski at an age in which most people have already decided to give it up. Her daily life in Switzerland rotated around the rhythms of luxury hotels; amidst their refined clientele, Coco never went unnoticed. Her white tweed suit and silk blouse with her ever-present strands of pearls attracted the attention of the ladies of high society, many of whom had been her clients in the past. She got up late in the morning and read fashion magazines or took long walks, often alone or with a chauffeured car following her at a walking pace.

Much of her energy was dedicated to renegotiating her agreement with the Société des Parfums, who managed the production and sales of Chanel fragrances. There had been a controversy between them for years that was finally settled in 1947, with a contract that awarded Coco 2% gross from the sales of all Chanel perfumes, making her one of the wealthiest women in the world. For many, it would have signified crossing the finishing line, but not for her. Being independently wealthy seemed like much too little for a woman like Coco Chanel.

Posing in her apartment in Rue Cambon for Vogue *magazine in 1954, Coco's elegant simplicity was impeccable, as always.*

She entertained the idea of writing her memoirs. It would not be a diary, but an autobiography that would require the help of an expert writer; but she immediately decided against enlisting her poet friend Reverdy, with whom she had had an intimate relationship. Then in Venice in the summer of 1947, she met the person she believed would be best for the job: Louise de Vilmorin, the author of a number of novels, and there was an immediate connection between them. They met again in Paris in September and reached an agreement for the division of rights to the book. In the long conversations that took place over the three following months, Coco recalled memories that Louise transformed into dense pages of text. The story focused on Coco's first twenty years of life, the ones that had left an indelible mark on the young Gabrielle's personality. In to her own words, "A childhood without affection created a strong need to be loved in me." Somewhere between recollections and inventions, the thread of her memory skipped over details that would have tarnished the image she had so carefully constructed of herself. The abyss between her current success and the secret misery of her infancy proved to be her greatest fragility. With that chasm looming before her as she narrated her past, she felt forced to put up walls to defend herself. She peppered the story of her younger years with invented details about how her father left the family to seek his fortune in America. Rather than revealing the desperation of being abandoned at the orphanage in Aubazine, she fabricated tales of other teachers and of strict but generous aunts who took her in after her mother's death. She made no mention of her past as a *poseuse* in the *café-chantant* in the company of army officers, or of the nuns in the orphanage. She confessed that "Lying was not difficult. Not only was I a liar by nature; my imagination, fueled by all kinds of bad novels, helped me embellish my lies and bring them to life with pathetic efforts." Yet the extraordinary tenacity that allowed her to leave such a miserable childhood behind was what made her successes so striking by contrast. Her lack of authenticity may have been the reason that American editors offered only a lukewarm response to her memoirs, which they courteously but resolutely rejected. The project ended in failure, as did the friendship between Coco and Louise.

The French novelist and screenwriter Louise de Vilmorin met Coco Chanel in 1947. Louise had once been engaged to Antoine de Saint-Exupéry and was later the lover of André Malraux.

Yards and yards of precious fabrics, full skirts, bustiers, and corsets were fundamental elements in Dior's style from the time it debuted in 1947.

In the meantime, fashion was changing. In 1947, an unknown stylist named Christian Dior presented a sensational collection of revolutionary garments that no longer strove for practicality but aimed instead to exalt the small-waisted feminine figure of women who were once again girdled in stays and corsets. The style, baptized by the enthusiastic editor of *Harper's Bazaar* as the "New Look," soon made its way around the world. Coco could not fathom the return of the corset, the success of the waist cincher, or the triumph of the corolla-shaped dresses. She exclaimed "Stylists have forgotten that there are women inside their dresses. How can anyone like those figures, dressed in brocade, that, when they sit down, look like an old Louis XIV armchair?"

Christian Dior in his Paris atelier, at work on his spring/summer collection in February 1957. Dior, the inventor of the New Look, died shortly afterward, in October of the same year.

"If a woman is shabbily dressed it's her dress that's noticed, but if she is impeccably dressed it's she who is noticed."

Perplexed by the rise of this new phenomenon, Coco decided to go to New York. She was a guest at the home of her friend Maggie Van Zuylen, where one evening she watched as Maggie's daughter was getting dressed to attend a prestigious debutante ball. She looked at the very expensive gown the girl planned to wear. It was the latest fashion, with a heart-shaped neckline and a strapless bodice held in place by a corset. She is said to have exclaimed "What a horror," before grabbing a scissors and a taffeta curtain and improvising a splendid gown that met with great success at the ball. "Dress shabbily and they remember the dress; dress impeccably and they remember the woman" was one of the life lessons Chanel gave to the young girl, who would later marry Guy de Rothschild. No one will ever know if this was the episode that gave Coco a change of heart, but we do know that while she was there on American turf, the desire and the project to become queen once again was born.

At 71, Coco decided to get back in the game, presenting 130 new designs to the overflow audience that attended her fashion show.

Mademoiselle, photographed in 1954 in Rue Cambon, ready for her comeback.

It was no coincidence that she had chosen to hold the event on February 5, 1954: five was her lucky number. She knew she was taking a risk, and she would take all the help she could get, even from her superstitions. She decided against using anonymous models, calling upon princesses and other celebrities to walk the runway in her creations. She was the first to realize the effectiveness of having brand ambassadors like the friends of her *protégé*, Marie-Hélène de Rothschild, the young woman who had inspired her return to the stage. Through her, Coco enlisted a group of young celebrities to model her creations, such as Maria-Eugénia Ouro Preto, who later married the poet Guy d'Arcangues; Princess Odile de Cröy, and Claude Pompidou, future wife of the French president. Coco ordered Pompidou's hair to be cut to bare her neck and her nape, which according to Coco were the most beautiful parts that a woman could reveal. In exchange for their formidable contacts, "*les blousons Chanel*," as the illustrious brigade came to be known, received all of Chanel's creations, in advance, to show off at the mundane events they attended.

When the fateful day finally arrived, the legendary golden chairs in Rue Cambon were packed with the most important people in the world of fashion: critics, journalists, old friends, long-established clients, and the *nouveaux riches* who only knew the Chanel name as a famous perfume. "Why did I come back? I was bored and it took me 15 years to realize it. I prefer disaster to nothingness," she confided to a journalist. The models walked the runway in a glacial silence while Coco stayed hidden in her usual position, sitting at the top of the stairs, surrounded by mirrors. Her return to the runway as a stubborn, proud, determined, surly woman of a certain age was met with a firing squad. European magazines crushed her under an avalanche of criticism, and Franco Zeffirelli, who was present at the event, recalled the press's reaction to the show as one of the cruelest experiences he had witnessed in his lifetime. Coco answered the critics with her silence and immediately went back to work in her Rue Cambon studio, where the huge halls on the second floor remained empty of clients. "Better," she told her seamstresses; "we have more room to get the new collection ready."

Marie-Hélène Arnaud, Coco's favorite model, wearing a black and white suit and a silk blouse designed by Chanel, in a photo published in Vogue *in 1959.*

Her true strength was her unvarying belief that she was on the right track; and time would prove that she was. The first to realize it were the Americans, where fashion magazines sensed that the return to Chanel's elegant comfort was a winning proposition and became a mouthpiece, heralding her triumphant return. *Vogue* dedicated a cover to Mademoiselle's favorite model, Marie-Hélène Arnaud, leaning nonchalantly against a wall with her hands in her pockets, dressed in a navy blue sheath dress that offered a glimpse of a white blouse with a black satin ribbon and the usual boater with Chanel ribbons. It was a no-frills look designed for comfort that exalted feminine beauty without constriction, a look conceived with the person who would wear it in mind, rather than the person who would see it. After all, Coco had always told her clients, "Before you leave the house, look in the mirror and take one thing off."

In 1955, *Life* magazine, the most influential women's magazine in the world at the time, also dedicated an article to the new Chanel collection, her third since she had reopened the doors of her atelier. The article was illustrated with photos of her new designs and reported that the woman behind the most famous perfume in the world was back on the scene and that her influence was already being felt worldwide. At 71, Chanel had lost none of her talent and had created far more than fashion: she had created a revolution.

With her modern, liberating fashion, Coco had once again freed women from the stereotypes of the times, sartorial and otherwise. Her style fulfilled the wishes of a new generation of independent women who voted, who earned their own living, and who had no time to waste, especially on choosing what to wear.

In a Chanel dress, women did not need to be twenty years old with a wasp waist to be fantastic. "My clothes make women look young," she claimed in an interview in *Vogue*. "Young girls are not the only beautiful women: in my opinion, women get more interesting after forty." Six months after the fashion show, the forerunner of the modern generation of supermodels, Suzy Parker, appeared on the cover of *Elle* magazine dressed to emulate Mademoiselle herself, in a tweed suit from the new collection. From that moment on, even the heartiest fans of the New Look in France changed their minds about it, and stylists adapted their styles accordingly, fluidifying shapes and softening waistlines. Chanel had won her bet.

Taking a break, surrounded by her Coromandel screens and the lavish decor of the apartment in Rue Cambon, after the successful Chanel fashion shows in 1957.

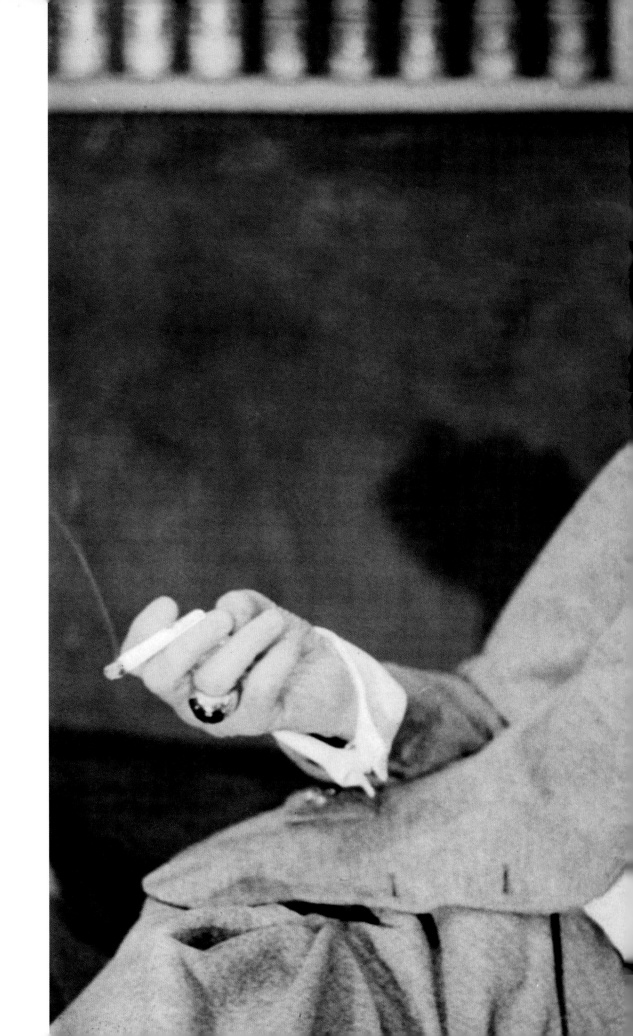

Coco Chanel used to say "A woman has the age she deserves." In this photo from 1962, she was nearing 80 but had not lost an ounce of her charm.

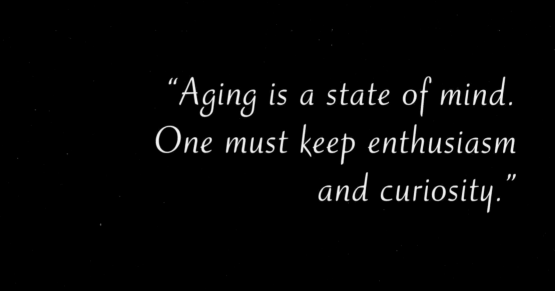

"*Aging is a state of mind. One must keep enthusiasm and curiosity.*"

Coco Chanel on the mirrored staircase in her atelier in 1954, the year of her comeback on the runways. This moment was captured by her friend, the American model Suzy Parker.

She had concerns about managing the finances of the empire she had rebuilt in record time, but a new contract with the Société des Parfumes, who managed the profits from her famous N° 5, put her mind at ease. On May 24, 1954, Coco sold her fashion house to the Société des Parfumes. In exchange, she remained the owner of Rue Cambon and received a substantial salary to direct the production of Chanel's *haute couture*, the style of which she held complete control over. In addition, the company paid all her expenses, including the suite at the Ritz, her Cadillac and the chauffeur that drove her around, her secretary, her meals, and even her stamps. She could finally dedicate herself to the only job that truly interested her: designing. Far from having depleted her energies, Mademoiselle, as she had become used to hearing herself called, still had many arrows in her quiver. She looked ten years younger, the wrinkles of her exile had disappeared, and her morale was soaring. "Nothing tires me more than a rest," she often repeated. She never started her day before noon, after having spent hours talking on the telephone as she lay in bed wearing her tailor-made white-silk men's pajamas. She delegated almost nothing: in fact, she personally chose all of her fabrics, one by one. She unrolled samples, crinkling them in her fingers to feel their consistency, and could choose the finest tweeds using only her sense of touch. Armed with her legendary scissors around her neck on a piece of string, she began to eliminate all that was unnecessary, like a sculptor in front of a block of marble. "Nobody knows how to tear fabric like Mademoiselle," whispered the seamstresses. She was perfectly aware of the theatricality of her performance with her scissors, and she used it often in the presence of journalists to impress them.

At work in the atelier to put the finishing touches on a chiffon evening gown, in the 1950s.

She sometimes stood for ten hours at a time while models worked in shifts, exhausted from hours of fittings. Videos filmed in the 1950s and 60s illustrated the way she worked. She was never seen designing. With her eyes sparkling from under her despotic straw boater, she used gestures to explain to the head tailors how they were to baste the patterns to the mannequins or directly on the models. Her workers followed her around without uttering a sound, passing her pins as she ripped a dress apart and reconstructed it, even twenty-five times, until it turned out perfectly—after which, with a move typical of a painter in front of the easel, she would step back to see it better. At 70, despite her arthritis, she was still spending hours kneeling in front of the models. Coco, who had never given in to anything, loved to bow before her dresses. At times, her hands hurt with the arthritis in her ring-covered fingers. She ate very little and drank only the occasional sip of water. She never took breaks and often worked late into the night, arriving well after 3 a.m. at her suite in the Ritz, where she could finally take off the boater she had been wearing all day.

Coco and her models in Rue Cambon, as she presented her new collection to the designers who would copy her creations, in 1957.

Top: a creation from the 1950s. "A woman can be overdressed but never over-elegant," Coco declared.

Right: Coco Chanel sitting on the steps of the atelier in Rue Cambon as she discusses the details of the fashion show with her collaborators, in 1954.

In 1955, she presented one of her most famous designs: the suit with the bordered, four-pocket jacket inspired by the military style, over a simple Tyrolean tunic similar to those she had seen on servants in a thermal station owned by Count Hubert von Pantz in Salzburg. Once again, she was preparing to give the world a new, indispensable livery for women, comparable only to her little black dress. Her new creation was a knit outfit that combined the shape of a man's sport suit and a woman's cardigan. Its light knitted fabric was unlined, to honor the less-is-more principle that Chanel had dictated to the entire world: "Always remove something, take something off. Don't ever add anything. Nothing is more beautiful than freedom of the body." It was like a uniform, and it probably reminded Coco of the years spent at the orphanage, where everyone was dressed the same way. It had the feel of a teenager's satisfaction when she gets her own way with the older ladies. Elegant during the day as well as in the evening, its hidden painstaking details give it an impeccably chic look. Despite its apparent simplicity, a Chanel suit is one of the highest forms of *haute couture*, requiring 150 hours of manual labor to make, with light, natural fabrics that are almost impossible to wrinkle. The jacket had no lapels. It had gold buttons and four front pockets, two on the chest and two on the hips, and it hid a secret that was suggested by the head tailors: a small chain sewn into the hem so that the coat would always hang perfectly. The final touch was the tone-on-tone trim on the borders. The skirt was just long enough to cover the knee, which made it comfortable to walk in, and it had a ribbon sewn to the inside of the waistband to attach to the blouse and keep it in place.

Chanel's iconic bouclé *wool suit with a short jacket with five pockets and a below-the-knee skirt, photographed in front of the display windows in Rue Cambon in 1959.*

On these pages, a model poses in Coco Chanel's apartment wearing two versions of her bordered suit, in the late 1950s.

Every bit of Chanel's style can be seen in this drawing by Cecil Beaton: the sleek suit, the pearls, the black straw hat, the two-tone slingback shoes, and the elegant décor of the apartment in Rue Cambon.

Right: in the 1950s, Coco was over 70 years old, but her figure was still perfect and she still looked like a model in her creations.

The new Chanel suit proved to be an unprecedented success that is still reproduced today, in every season and in an infinity of variations, but always with the same unaltered structure. Women from all over the world competed to get one, including queens and princesses who chose the iconic suit for their public appearances. Jacqueline Kennedy was wearing one on November 22, 1963, as she rode through the streets of Dallas in a convertible limousine with her husband, President John F. Kennedy. She was later photographed at the inauguration of Lyndon Johnson aboard Air Force One, wearing the same strawberry pink Chanel suit, stained with the blood of her husband who had been assassinated only hours before.

In another of her unpredictable gestures, ten years after the launch of the suit, Coco gave the rights to reproduce the design to some American garment manufacturers. With one clip of the scissors, she had cut through social distinctions, transforming artisanal hand tailoring into the modern empire of *prêt-à-porter*. The revolutionary importance of this move was immeasurable, and in just a few years the Chanel suit was being mass-produced. In the mid-1960s, seven suits out of ten were Chanel copies, but she knew that the suit would have been copied, with or without her permission. She did not care. "All that you find is meant to be taken," she claimed. She considered plagiarism the most splendid form of homage.

President John F. Kennedy and his wife Jackie, who is wearing a strawberry pink Chanel suit, as they arrived at the Dallas airport on November 22, 1963, the day the president was assassinated.

In 1955, she launched another timeless classic, her 2.55 bag. Its shape was the reinterpretation of a bag in grosgrain-trimmed jersey that she had created for herself in the late 1920s, inspired by the military shoulder bag. At the time, women did not use shoulder bags, but that was one of the rules that Coco had no respect for, stating "I was tired of having to keep my bag in my hand all the time and tired of losing it, so I put a strap through it and put it over my shoulder." Redesigned with modern femininity in mind, her new creation was made to be a woman's best friend, where

she could keep her secrets, so she recuperated a functional element from her original model, a double flap. The larger one served to close the bag and cover a hidden pocket made to hold a few banknotes to use as tips—or, as Mademoiselle called them, "small change to spend on small comforts"—while the smaller flap served to cover three compartments, one of which was made specifically to hold lipstick.

The sturdy shoulder strap was threaded through two holes. It was made of a metal chain interlaced with leather. "Believe me, I know women. Give them chains, women love chains." Women did love Chanel's chains, because rather than imprison them, her chains freed them, or at least their hands.

Chanel made the revolutionary decision to propose a daywear version made with the identical pattern, in addition to the evening version in jersey and silk. It had to be sturdy but elegant, so she chose to make it in soft lambskin that was quilted in a diamond pattern to give it more structure and consistency. It is believed that the *matelassé* pattern, which would become another of the brand's trademarks, was inspired by the checkered jackets of the stable grooms that she had often seen during her affair with Boy. From the moment it was created, it became the most copied woman's bag in the world, capacious but easy to carry. Initially, it was produced only in the colors Coco had chosen for her own wardrobe: navy blue, beige, black, and brown.

The name of the 2.55 bag refers to the date it was first produced, February 1955. In 1988, Karl Lagerfeld replaced the original rectangular latch, known as the "Mademoiselle lock," with the brand's logo of two interlocked Cs, which came to be known as the "double C lock."

In 1965, Chanel presented breathtaking evening outfits made with glittered tweed and embroidered fabrics, like this creation in metallic silk.

In 1964, she expanded her collections to include women's trousers, a fashion that she herself had helped launch in her youth. With embroidered silk and sequined tweeds, she created soft, wide-legged evening pants combined with sleeveless tunics inspired by the garments of China and Tibet, in colors that mixed all the shades of nature, from golden yellow to green. Around the same time, she declared war on the miniskirt launched by the English stylist Mary Quant, who had the insight to choose models like Twiggy, a slight little girl who met none of the era's classic standards of beauty. Mademoiselle was at the height of her success and did nothing to hide her disgust when she declared "It's awful to see those knees." She later clarified that her aversion certainly had nothing to do with the scandal of revealing a few inches of bare skin. Rather, she said, it was all about the fact that the skirt revealed what she considered one of the least graceful parts of the female body, the knee; but in reality, at a deeper level, she knew that a woman who gave up her modesty lost her charm.

The model, Marisa Berenson, granddaughter of Coco's archrival, Elsa Schiaparelli, wearing an embroidered mauve lamé suit composed of an Indian tunic and a pair of shorts that were Chanel's alternative to the miniskirt.

In 1957, Chanel created the two-tone slingback shoe. She considered it apt for every occasion, stating "You leave in the morning wearing beige and black, you have lunch in beige and black, and you attend a cocktail party wearing beige and black. You're dressed for the entire day!"

One of the Oriental-inspired bracelets created by Chanel in the 1960s. In contrast to the simple elegance of her clothes, her fashion jewelry designs were always bold and theatrical.

As usual, Coco completed every design with costume jewelry that, given its limited cost, could be renewed with every season. Crosses, pins, gold buttons, and the ever-present six strands of pearls became an integral part of the Chanel look. When her assistants brought her trays full of pieces, just as they had done in the 1930s, Coco took them by the handful and, with her impeccable taste, carefully chose the pieces that would create the perfect combination with her suits. Accessories were a fundamental style element, but shoes had become the new status symbol. After all, according to Coco, "A woman with good shoes is never ugly." She became a liberator once again, this time from the discomfort of spike heels, when she designed her famous two-tone slingback pump. It had a low block heel and a gold toe for eveningwear, or a black toe for the day. It was created in the 1960s in collaboration with the expert French shoemaker Raymond Massaro, the same man that, years earlier, she had entrusted with her secret of using work to forget life's displeasures. He followed Mademoiselle's instructions and, after much fine-tuning, the revolutionary design of this closed-toe, open-heel beige shoe succeeded in making a woman's feet look smaller and her legs look longer. Jewelry and shoes were the embodiment of the perfect harmony with artisans that Coco had pursued her entire life, probably because the artisans reminded her of the love for honesty and for a job well done that she had been assimilating since childhood. Her early memories of the hardworking life of the countryside that she traveled with her father in his peddler's cart, and of the long days spent watching the fervor of weavers and carders, of potters and nail-makers, would instill a deep respect for artisans and the quality of their crafts forever in her heart.

In 1957, Neiman Marcus, one of the most famous department stores in the United States, awarded Chanel the title of "the most influential designer of the century." Two years later, the interlocking Cs became the brand's official symbol, reproduced everywhere, on the gold buttons of its suits, on the labels of its perfumes, on the leather of its bags, and on the buckles of its belts.

At the height of her glory, Coco met Luchino Visconti, an encounter that stunned them both. He was thirty and was fascinated by her rare combination of "feminine beauty, masculine intelligence, and fantastic energy." Swept away by his culture, she followed him on a series of trips to Italy. He introduced her to his family in Milan, then took her to Venice, Rome, and Capri, where Coco returned many times, intoxicated with the colors and fragrances of the island. Her infallible intuition told her that Visconti possessed true talent, so she put in a good word for him with Jean Renoir, who chose him as an assistant in his movie *Les Bas-fonds*. It was the beginning of a brilliant career and of his rise to fame in the world of international cinema. Her encounter with Visconti strengthened her ties to movie production that had begun in Hollywood with the partnership that Sam Goldwyn had so desired in the 1930s. This time it was the directors of Nouvelle Vague that sought her collaboration. Louis Malle asked her to design the costumes for Jeanne Moreau in his 1958 production of *Les Amants,* and she dressed Delphine Seyrig in a series of ethereal black and white costumes in Alain Resnais's movie *Last Year at Marienbad*. The following year, when she met her friend Visconti again and he asked her to create Romy Schneider's wardrobe for his movie *Boccaccio '70*, she produced a series of outfits that were unmistakably Chanel. He also asked Coco to give the young actress a more sophisticated style; Schneider was twenty-two at the time and had earned her fame playing the role of Sissi, the young empress of Austria. It was the beginning of an important relationship, marked by wool *bouclé* outfits, open-heel, two-toned sandals, and pearl necklaces. Another of Chanel's icons appeared in the 1968 movie *Rosemary's Baby*, in which Mia Farrow is seen with various versions of the famous 2.55 bag on her shoulder. But Chanel's liaison with the world of cinema went beyond the movies to conquer the personal wardrobes of many stars, including Elizabeth Taylor, Jane Fonda, Annie Girardot, and Brigitte Bardot. She became friends with Anouk Aimée and discussed literature with Jeanne Moreau as the list of stars who chose her creations grew along with her fame.

Coco is giving the finishing touches to Romy Schneider's look in the atelier in Rue Cambon in 1960. When they met for the first time, Mademoiselle was 77 and the actress was 22. They took an immediate liking to each other and became lifelong friends.

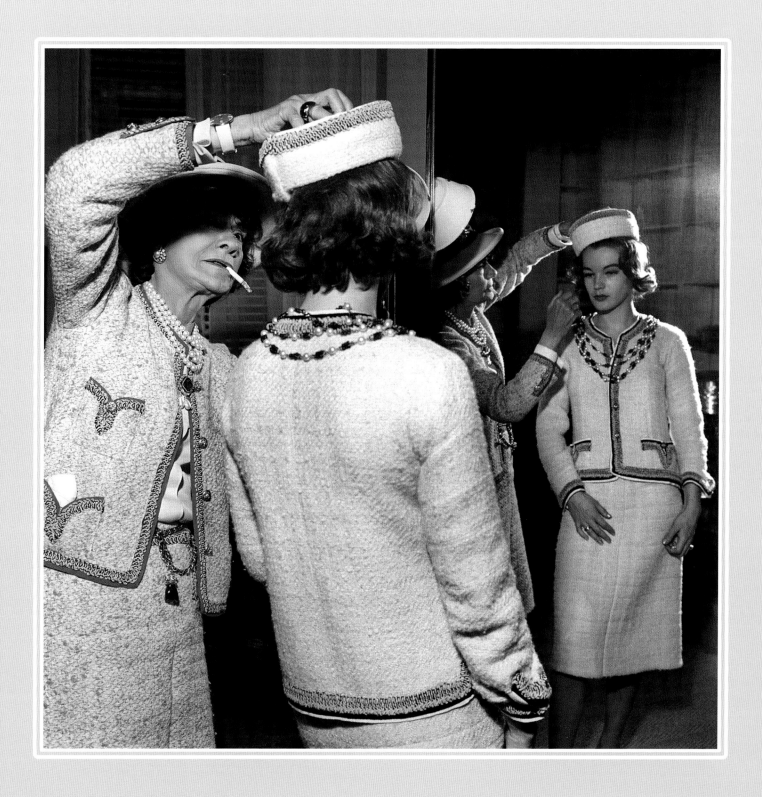

Over time, Coco's character, forged by adversity as much as her successes, became increasingly imperious. During the interviews she gladly consented to, she revealed all of her extraordinary charisma, cheerfully and spontaneously responding to the curiosity of the journalists who besieged her; but when their questions were too trite, her answers were cutting. When she was asked "What do you usually eat?" she answered, "A gardenia in the morning and a rose at night"; or to the question "How old are you?" she replied "Either a hundred or zero, depending on the day." When a journalist pointed out that hers was one of the most copied styles, she answered with her usual verve: "When I see some of the outfits that have supposedly been inspired by Chanel, I strongly protest. I can guarantee that among my creations, there is not even one potato sack." Even with her friends, she continuously switched from generous impulses to stubborn spite, inviting them to dinner night after night for weeks and them forgetting about them for months. Anyone who refused her invitation, even if it was last-minute, was in trouble. She never had a good relationship with the other stylists, and she detested the dominance of men in a sector destined to women. The only men whose styles she found interesting were Cristobal Balenciaga, who she considered a great talent, and Yves Saint-Laurent, who she said "has excellent taste. The more he copies me, the better taste he displays." Her critics were naturally among those she targeted with her sharp-witted comments. Liane Viaguié, one of the models at Rue Cambon, recalled how Coco described the unpleasant encounters with fashion journalists she had to endure at the fashion shows: "They showed up at every fashion show in droves, shabbily dressed and shabbily groomed, completely without femininity and at times even foul-smelling, which is certainly not pleasant. They're fat and ugly and they're envious of my models' wasp waists and of the women who can afford to buy my *haute couture*. But the thing I find reproachable, above everything else, is that they criticize the wrong things, which is normal when you don't know what you're talking about."

A portrait from the 1960s. The passing years added to Coco's charm. She declared "Elegance is not the prerogative of those who have just escaped from adolescence, but of those who have already taken possession of their future."

Unlike them, she was always perfect, dressed in her uniform of a beige linen suit with braided red and blue trim and a cascade of both costume and authentic jewelry. In her pocket, she always kept a white cotton handkerchief steeped in her perfume that announced her arrival at the atelier.

Even in the last years of her life, she insisted on looking impeccable, so she received the makeup artist Jacques Clemente in her suite at the Ritz every morning. He was just twenty, but he was already well known; in fact, as soon as he finished with Mademoiselle, he rushed off to his next client, the duchess of Windsor. At their first encounter, she put him to the test, asking him to soften the shiny black of her eyes, which over the years had become two piercing ebony colored slivers.

She detested gray hair on women and hid her own with hair dyes and the classic straw boater that she sometimes used as a tool to free herself from boring visitors. "I can always point to my hat and say that I was just going out."

Mademoiselle in front of the Chanel perfume boutique in the Rue Cambon, in the early 1960s.

Coco Chanel in 1962, impeccable in a black and white suit with her Noget scissors hanging from a piece of packing string around her neck. "If I had to choose an insignia, I would like it to be my scissors."

Coco Chanel at work, photographed by Douglas Kirkland in 1962.

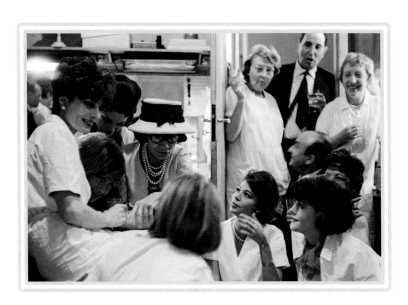

Coco in the middle of seamstresses and models in the atelier in Rue Cambon in 1962. She never sketched her designs. Instead, she used gestures to explain to the head tailors how they were to baste the patterns as she went on cutting and pinning for hours, until she obtained the result she had in mind.

Coco as she adjusts a dress on one of her models. Her arthritis caused sharp pains in her hands, but before every fashion show she worked relentlessly, sometimes standing for 10 hours straight.

Right: Giving the finishing touches to a suit, before a photo shoot.

Photographed by Douglas Kirkland on the legendary Rue Cambon staircase, where she could sit and watch the runway show without being seen and observe the audience's reactions in the reflection of the mirrors.

A model in an organza evening gown walks down the stairs at the spring/summer fashion show in 1963.

Coco Chanel sitting on the sofa at Rue Cambon with the baroness
Rothschild and, in the middle, the French actress Anouk Aimée,
during a photo shoot that was published in Vogue in 1966.

Top: Coco with Francine Weisweiller, a French socialite and
a friend of Cocteau's.

At 82, ten years after her triumphant return to the runways of Chanel, Coco was extremely wealthy once again. She drew up her will that year, expressing her desire to leave her assets to CoGa (which stood for Coco Gabrielle), a financial holding company that would, among other things, oversee the annuities with which Coco had always supported young artists in times of need. A substantial amount of money was left to the orphanage in Aubazine that had taken her in as a child. She still worked tirelessly, but every now and then she was overwhelmed with solitude. Many of her friends had died, her family had never been important to her, and her favorite nephew only came to see her when he needed money. She stayed at the atelier late into the night, going back to her desolately empty suite as late as possible. She often said "I don't regret anything in my life except the things I didn't do." This from a woman who, in her life, had done a myriad of things but who still felt she had much more to give.

On the day her funeral was celebrated in the Madeleine Church in Paris, all of the wreaths were white except the one from Luchino Visconti, which had three red roses among the camellias. She was buried in Lausanne, under a marble gravestone carved with five lions' heads, her lucky number and her zodiac sign. After a fairytale life, she died in an instant at the Ritz in Paris. It was January 10, 1971, a Sunday, the day of the week she detested because it forced her to be idle, which was inconceivable for a woman who had made work her reason to live.

At 88, Coco still worked tirelessly every day with the spirit of a warrior and the tenacity that accompanied her through her entire life.

A Legendary Perfume

Chanel N° 5 was created at the beginning of the 1920s, and it has been seducing the world ever since. On display at the MoMA like a work of art, it is a timeless icon that has inspired the likes of Dalí and Andy Warhol. It is the scent of the movie stars of today and yesterday, made even more legendary by Marilyn Monroe when she was asked "What do you wear to bed?" to which she answered "Nothing but a few drops of Chanel N° 5."

A century has gone by since its launch on May 5, 1921, but Chanel N° 5 is still widely perceived as the perfume *par excellence*, the one everyone knows about, even those who have never used it. It has stood up to time and to fashion's passing whims, as if Coco Chanel had found the formula for eternal femininity. In numerology, the number 5, her lucky number, symbolizes the transcendence to a superior state. She considered the number so significant that she selected it as the date to present her collections and repeatedly used it as a decorative element, on buttons, between the stones in her costume jewelry, and even in her apartment in Rue Cambon where it appeared in the least expected places, such as in the rock-crystal drops of her chandeliers.

The iconic N° 5 bottle. With its minimalist lines, it made design history and it has been on display since 1959 in the permanent collections of the Museum of Modern Art in New York.

American soldiers lined up in front of the Chanel shop in Paris, waiting to buy a bottle of N° 5 to take home to their girlfriends, right after the Liberation.

From the time it was created, Chanel N° 5 represented an epic turning point in the world of perfumes; even today, it is one of the most sought-after scents in the world, said to be sold at the amazing pace of one bottle every 55 seconds.

In the 1920s, after the commotion it caused in Paris, women competed with one another to snatch up the new fragrance, making it an object of desire in the rest of Europe too; but its true success arrived in the 1950s, when it took the United States by storm.

Female soldiers choosing perfumes in the shop in the Rue Cambon. After 1945, demand for Chanel N° 5 in the United States rocketed, sales increasing tenfold.

The American soldiers who arrived in Paris by the thousands during the Liberation in 1944 stood in line in front of Chanel's shop to buy the perfect souvenir to take to their sweethearts at home across the ocean. It was not long before the perfume was distributed tax-free at the exchanges on military posts, and the bottle that embodied the essence of French luxury suddenly became accessible to the middle classes at a discount price. As a result, the unmistakable scent of N° 5 wafted over every corner of the earth.

As the perfume's commercial success grew, its distinctive bottle became a social and cultural symbol. Coco had conceived it as an avant-garde sculpture, and it was no surprise that its unusual, essential, boxy shape was met with the enthusiasm of artists. The first to make it the subject of one of his drawings was the French illustrator Sem, who had already portrayed Coco in a number of his caricatures in newspapers. In 1921, in recognition of the perfume's success, he depicted it in a sketch (which is sometimes mistakenly thought to be an advertisement) of a young girl, dressed and coiffed in perfect Chanel style, as she gazes up at a giant bottle of N° 5. He published a second illustration that depicts the stylist as she works in her atelier, framed by the outline of the famous perfume bottle. Two decades later, Salvador Dalí paid tribute to his friend Coco's creation with a work entitled *The Essence of Dalí*, in which a bottle with a rectangular outline similar to that of N° 5 sports a beautiful, ironically self-deprecating mustache like the one he drew on Leonardo's *Mona Lisa*. Some of the most famous works of art tied to the fragrance belong to a series of prints by Andy Warhol. The prints were a pop-art reinterpretation of the advertisements that appeared between 1954 and 1956, entitled *Ads: Chanel*. In the collective imagination, the N° 5 bottle had become an icon of style and a piece of history such that in 1959, it earned a spot in the permanent collections of the Museum of Modern Art in New York.

Left: Chanel N° 5 appeared for the first time in an illustration by Sem dated 1921, with the unmistakable outline of the minimalist bottle designed by Coco.

Top: The Essence of Dalí, *a work by Dalí that pays tribute to Coco Chanel's perfume in a 1954 photo by Philippe Halsman. According to the painter, "Of the five senses, the sense of smell is incontestably the one that best conveys a sense of immortality."*

On the following pages: Ads: Chanel, *a series of prints by Andy Warhol from 1985 that presents a pop-art version of the 1950s perfume advertisements.*

The rest is history, but business as well, because with a drop of perfume and her extraordinary foresight, Mademoiselle Chanel had transformed the brand into a giant in a system that combined the lucrative world of cosmetics with the world of fashion. N° 5 was soon followed by many other Chanel perfumes: N° 22 in 1922 and, in the years immediately after, *Gardénia*, *Bois des Îles*, *Cuir de Russie*, *Sycomore*, *Une idée,* and *Jasmin*. *Pour Monsieur* was launched in 1955, and the last perfume to be presented under Coco's control was N° 19, in 1970.

As she expanded the range of her fragrances, Coco turned to the power of advertising to consolidate the success of N° 5. She herself was the first to lend her face, photographed by François Kollar in her suite at the Ritz in Paris. The image of Mademoiselle dressed in a fabulous black dress in pure Chanel style as she leaned on her fireplace was published for the first time in *Harper's Bazaar* in 1937. But what would change everything was the extraordinary publicity that Marilyn Monroe unwittingly offered for free, in 1952, when a rather indiscreet journalist from *Life* magazine asked her what she wore to bed and she answered "Nothing but a few drops of Chanel N° 5." Sales soared, and the perfume that was already the most famous in the world became legend. Monroe had an unbreakable bond with the French *eau de parfum,* and it became even stronger with a series of photos taken on March 24, 1955. Marilyn was more beautiful than ever, posed in her hotel room with the legendary bottle, before attending the premiere of Tennessee Williams's play *Cat on a Hot Tin Roof* at the Morosco Theater in New York. She was depicted again with the famous bottle in a series of photos for *Modern Screen* magazine that portrayed her scandalously naked on her bed, but the photos were never published.

Marilyn Monroe with a bottle of N° 5 in the famous photo taken by Ed Feingersh in 1955.

Since then, Chanel's ads for its iconic perfume have always featured beautiful stars with an innate elegance, shot by photographers capable of making them even more fascinating. N° 5 has an inimitable bouquet that is persistent and sensual but with a decisive character, a bouquet that over the years has been associated with the strong emblematic women who have loved it and left its *sillage* in their wake, sweet and sensuous like soft feminine curves. In 1968, Lauren Hutton, the famous star of Robert Altman's *A Wedding* and costar with Richard Gere in *American Gigolo*, posed in an ad shot by Richard Avedon as she jumped in the air in a fabulous pink suit with knee-length shorts. Later, Catherine Deneuve, the refined French actress who starred in *Belle de Jour*, was chosen to represent the perfume in a series of advertising campaigns directed by Helmut Newton and Richard Avedon. Carole Bouquet became Chanel's favorite celebrity for television advertising. She starred in two commercials, one directed by Ridley Scott and another, in the 1990s, directed by Bettina Rheims titled *Sentiment Troublant*, in which she reads a monologue from the movie *Gilda*. Patrick Demarchelier was chosen to take the photos that flooded newspapers and magazines.

The French actress Carole Bouquet photographed by Patrick Demarchelier for the 1993 ad campaign.

On the following page: Catherine Deneuve in a photo by Richard Avedon for a 1972 ad campaign destined exclusively for the American market.

Catherine Deneuve for Chanel

N°5

N°5
CHANEL
PARIS

PARFUM

NORDSTROM

Among the brand's most memorable advertising campaigns was a commercial made by the movie director Luc Besson. Based on a storyboard illustrated by Milo Manara and shot in the Cinecittà Studios in Rome, it starred Estella Warren as Little Red Riding Hood, determined to tame the wolf. Another prestigious commercial, directed by Baz Luhrmann, was reminiscent of his famous movie *Moulin Rouge*, starring Nicole Kidman. Kidman appears in the commercial in a Karl Lagerfeld gown cut low on her back where a N° 5 pendant made with 687 diamonds hangs. Among the more recent campaigns, one of the commercials that stands out is titled *Train de Nuit*, created by the director of the movie *Amélie*, Jean Pierre Jeunet. The commercial starred Audrey Tautou in dreamlike scenes set on the Orient Express. In 2012, Chanel surprised everyone when it enlisted the actor Brad Pitt, the first male ambassador of the quintessential women's perfume.

Nicole Kidman, photographed by Baz Luhrmann for a 2005 Chanel N° 5 ad.
On the following page: Audrey Tatou, photographed by Dominique Issermann in 2009.

Fashion Fades, Only Style Remains the Same

The legend of Coco. A friend to Picasso and Cocteau and a discreet patron of artists and poets, Coco left an indelible mark on the history of fashion and much more. She inspired movies and short films that starred actresses such as Shirley MacLaine, Geraldine Chaplin, Anna Mouglalis, and Audrey Tautou.

The writer André Malraux predicted that "From this century in France, three names will remain: de Gaulle, Picasso, and Chanel." And he was right. Coco's legacy traveled well beyond France and marked not only one era, but triumphantly crossed into the new millennium as well. Today, Chanel is a global empire with over 200 international boutiques that churn out billions of euros in sales every year in a number of branches of the fashion industry: clothing, watches, jewelry, and cosmetics. The brand's main headquarters at the corner of Rue Cambon and Rue Saint-Honoré in Paris have become one of the most iconic locations of the French capital, a must-see for anyone visiting the city.

When Mademoiselle passed away in 1971, her work continued under her assistants Gaston Berthelot and Ramon Esparza, and later passed under the direction of Karl Lagerfeld, who affiliated his name with the brand and guided it into the new century. As creative director, he was responsible for the brand's *prêt-à-porter, haute couture,* and accessory lines and managed to modernize the fashion house's style codes without ever betraying Coco's vision. Using respect and creativity, he preserved the soul of her work, playing with timeless iconic elements like *bouclé* fabrics, small jackets with no lapels, bags with chain shoulder straps, pearls, and camellias.

Karl Lagerfeld, the creative director for Chanel from 1983 to 2019, is seen here at the Grand Palais in Paris in October 2013 during the fashion week runway shows.

In 2005, the Grand Palais, the symbol of Parisian modernity, became the venue for Chanel's runway events. Chanel was the exclusive sponsor for the restoration of the majestic building.

Lagerfeld presented the new creations on the amazing sets he invented for the Chanel fashion shows, which have been held every season at the Grand Palais in Paris since 2005. Inspired by a casino, a Paris street, a supermarket, a forest, an 18th-century Mediterranean garden, an ocean liner, an airport, and even the Eiffel Tower, the scenic design changed every time, transforming the glass pavilion that had been built for the *Exposition Universelle* of 1900 into a runway, where his creations evoked bewitching dreams and adventurous tales. With all this, he succeeded in seducing the guests and making the photographers lose their minds while always keeping the focus on the clothes, just as Coco had wanted. "My job isn't to do what she did, but what she could have done. Chanel is an idea that we can reinterpret endlessly," declared Lagerfeld. He worked for the brand for 36 years, until the end of his long career.

The glass-and-iron structure of the Grand Palais covers more than 13,000 square meters, where spectacular stages that change with each fashion show are created. In the photo above, the naïf-style jungle of imaginary plants created for the presentation of the 2015 spring/summer haute couture *collection.*

The Chanel trademark is a legend of *haute couture,* but Coco's legacy goes far beyond fashion. While some people turn everything they touch into gold, she turned everything she touched into legend. She was an extraordinary woman who was not just a genius of style and an acute businesswoman; she is also remembered as one of the most influential patrons of new art forms of her time.

Yet, apart from a pair of andirons signed by the sculptor Jacques Lipchitz and a small painting by Dalí, no works of art, no signed portraits, not even a painting by the great masters she associated with adorned her walls. Her love for artists went beyond their art; she had no other desire than to be dazzled by them, and nothing made her prouder than to be able to discover them, to get to know them intimately, much better than any collector could ever have done. Coco believed that the fascination of art was in the moment of its creation, a concept that coincides with her immense respect for everything handmade, from the one-of-a-kind pieces created by the brand's excellent suppliers to her exquisite Coromandel screens.

The consideration that she had for the writers and artists with whom she loved to surround herself revealed her intelligence and critical sense and her ability to understand talent instinctively, despite not having had much formal instruction. She loved art and art loved her. The times she worked hand in hand with painters, musicians, ballerinas, and writers were countless. We have narrated in previous chapters how, from a simple spectator, she became a star on the Parisian scene, creating costumes for the performances of the Ballets Russes that sprang from the imagination of Serge Diaghilev. She was so susceptible to the charms of the artists she met during the course of her long life that many chance meetings, like those with Stravinsky and Picasso, became lifelong friendships. With some, it was a matter of would-be love affairs, while with others it was a relationship suspended between admiration and rivalry. "Chanel's originality was the opposite of mine," said Salvador Dalí, the surrealist painter who inspired the bold decorations for the dresses created by Coco's rival Elsa Schiaparelli, including the famous lobster printed on a skirt of pure white silk. "I have always shamelessly exhibited my thoughts, while she neither conceals hers nor shows them off, but instead dresses them up. She has the best dressed body and soul on earth." Her enormous respect for literature and poetry are evident in the words regarding her poet friend Reverdy, whom she considered immortal. "Poets are not like us. They never die

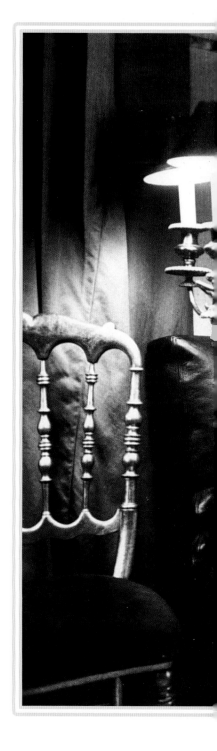

Coco Chanel with the writer, playwright, and intimate friend Jean Cocteau. Coco designed the costumes for his ballet Le Train Bleu *in 1924, as well as for six other theater productions.*

completely." The admiration she felt for them was reciprocated by writers like Jean Cocteau, who wrote in a letter to Coco "Your work is a kind of miracle. You have worked in fashion according to rules that would seem to have value only for painters, musicians, and poets."

In fondly describing her, he said "Her fits of rage, her harshness, her fabulous jewelry, her creations, her whims, her extreme behaviors, her kindnesses like her sense of humor and her generosity make up a unique character, intriguing, attractive and repelling at the same time, excessive. In a word, human."

Colette also penned a portrait of her in *Prisons et Paradis*. "The sweetness that Chanel demands and obtains from herself surprises me more than her authority, having read what is most readable on her face: her two long despotic black eyebrows that she never plucks, that are capable of coming together, of going up and going down (especially down), flinching every time her wavy bangs disturb them. My attention goes from those eyebrows down to her mouth, but there I can't easily make up my mind, because in her moments of concentration and displeasure, the middle of her face seems to become concave, sucked in from the inside, retreating under the overhang of her brows and the coils of her black hair. It's only an instant, but one of total muteness, of fierce withdrawal, a fleeting inertness from which the mouth suddenly recovers. Sinuous lips with sad impatient corners, kept in check by sharp teeth."

A famous reporter, Maurice Sachs, also described her: "She was not a classic beauty but she was irresistible. Her words were not dazzling but her heart and her spirit made her unforgettable."

A portrait of Coco at the time of her comeback on the runways in 1954. Photo by Horst P. Horst.

These snapshots made of words correspond to the many images that depict her. Some were pencil sketches signed by artists like Feliks Topolksi or the satirical illustrator Sem, but most were photos, because Coco Chanel was one of the most photographed people of her time. In the early 1930s, when she first visited the studios in Hollywood, she had learned the secrets of being photogenic and she wore her creations with natural elegance, like a model. In fact, it was often rightly said that no one could wear Chanel like Chanel. She loved being in the spotlight, sure of herself and confident in the taste that had earned her the crown as queen of elegance for as long as she lived. She knew well that if she charmed the photographers, their photos of her designs for the fashion magazines would be more striking; but above all, she knew, before all of the other stylists, that her own image would be a fundamental ingredient in the brand's success. Her face often appeared alongside her clothes in magazines, photographed by masters such as Horst (pseudonym of Paul Albert Bohrmann), a pioneer of fashion photography as an expression of elegance, style, and glamour. In 1937, he took a close-up of her in her favorite armchair in Rue Cambon.

Chanel photographed by Horst P. Horst in 1937, on the beige satin bergère *armchair in the entryway of her apartment in Rue Cambon.*

"Everything I do is driven by passion."

Hoyningen-Huene, who took legendary photos of Chanel designs that were published in *Vogue*, portrayed her in an iconic head-and-shoulders shot, wearing a white lace collar that resembled a Renaissance ruff, with her deep dark eyes standing out under the imperious arch of her eyebrows, ready to pierce her observers. Few people knew that those eyes had a hard time focusing because she hid her nearsightedness from everyone. Her glasses rarely appeared in photos, but they can be seen in the photo in Rue Cambon, lying on her desk. She always kept them at hand, together with her cigarettes, in the spacious pockets of her suits. She was not often seen smoking, but the surrealist photographer Man Ray captured her in profile, strong and rebellious with a cigarette between her lips, in a shot that synthesizes the ideal association between her face, her body, and the style of her character.

An intense portrait of Coco taken in the 1930s by George Hoyningen-Huene. At the time, the photographer was the representative of the American edition of Vogue *in Paris. Born in St. Petersburg, he fled Russia during the revolution in 1917.*

Boris Lipnitzki, the photographer of the stars, portrayed her in a splendid full-length shot; but she was particularly fond of the snapshots taken by photo reporter Roger Schall, who captured her more than once with her artist friends: at dinner in Monte Carlo with Salvador Dalí and Georges Auric as she entertained them with one of her anecdotes, dressed as a tree at the Forest Ball, sitting on a branch in the gardens of Villa La Pausa, or as she chatted with Igor Stravinsky. Other famous portraits were taken by Robert Doisneau, who got a shot of her infinitely reflected image in mirrors on the steps of Rue Cambon, and by Douglas Kirkland, who took her photo when she was almost 80 years old in 1962 and declared that "Her legs look like those of a young girl." Another famous photo of Coco was taken in 1964 by Henri Cartier-Bresson as she sat on her sofa in Rue Cambon; and Cecil Beaton, the photographer of the Queen of England, took a series of magnificent portraits, including the ones he shot in her apartment in 1966.

Coco Chanel in 1937, in a shot taken by Boris Lipnitzki, surrounded by the precious Coromandel screens that she had collected for years and that she scattered around her apartment to create marvelous movable walls.

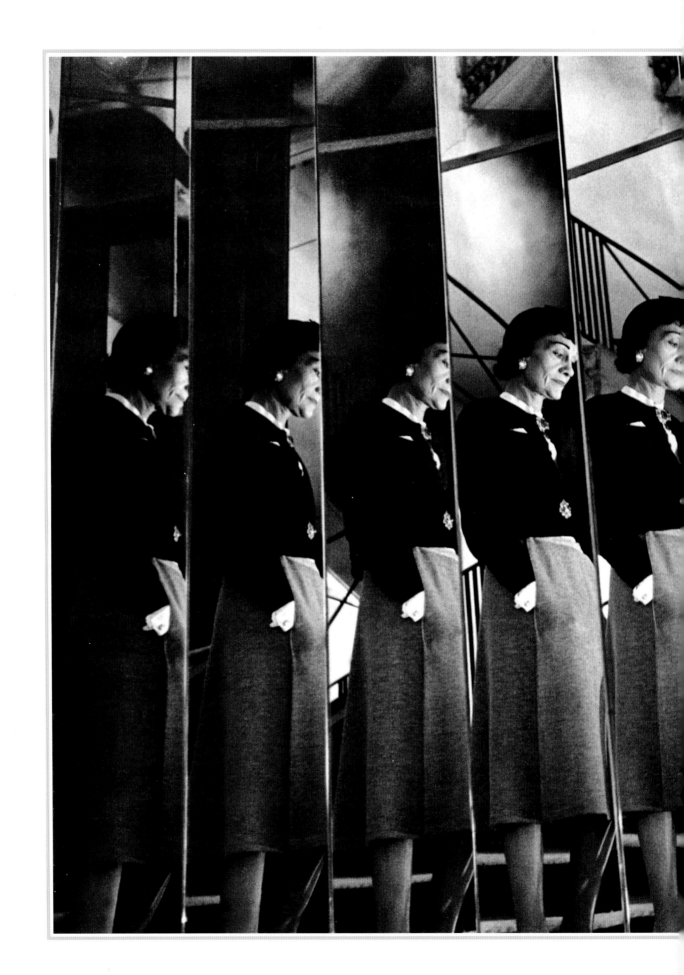

In this famous photo by Robert Doisneau, taken in 1953, Chanel is reflected in the infinity mirrors on the staircase of the Rue Cambon apartment, where she sat, unobserved, to watch all the runway shows.

Cecil Beaton also created the costumes for *Coco*, the Broadway musical that told the story of her life. The costumes won a Tony Award, but Coco was unable to reach New York for the premiere of the musical on December 18, 1969, due to a paralysis in her hand that lasted for two months.

Although she had always defended her privacy and was constantly on the lookout for indiscretions or intrusions into her private life, she entrusted the production to Alan Lerner and Frederick Brisson without ever asking to approve the script before it reached the stage, where it ran for 329 performances. Katharine Hepburn played Coco during the time when she had just returned to the *haute couture* runway after 15 years of absence. Reviews were mediocre, but the performances on tour were sold out in many cities. The success may have been due in part to the brilliant idea of closing each performance with a sensational runway show of Chanel's most beautiful creations from 1918 to 1959.

Chanel's legend has also been immortalized in movies. Her extraordinary story has inspired television producers and movie directors who were charmed by this woman who had lived a thousand unconventional lives. Coco was played by the great actress Shirley MacLaine in the 2008 television movie *Coco Chanel*. The movie narrates the story of Gabrielle from her early childhood to the twilight of her life, when she uses romantic flashbacks to reveal little-known details about the glories and dramas of her life.

The actress Katharine Hepburn played Chanel in the musical Coco *that opened on Broadway in 1969. The costumes for the musical, over 250 garments inspired by the Chanel style, were created by the photographer and costume designer Cecil Beaton, who won two Academy Awards for* Gigi *and* My Fair Lady.

In the 2008 Italian television series Coco Chanel, *the Oscar winner Shirley MacLaine played Coco. "I've been a big fan of her creations since the 1950s; my friend Audrey Hepburn told me about her and now I can't believe I got to play her," said the actress.*

HAUT ET COURT, CINE @ ET WARNER BROS. PICTURES PRESENTENT

AUDREY TAUTOU

BENOÎT POELVOORDE   ALESSANDRO NIVOLA
MARIE GILLAIN   EMMANUELLE DEVOS

COCO AVANT CHANEL

UN FILM DE ANNE FONTAINE

UN FILM DE ANNE FONTAINE SCENARIO ANNE FONTAINE ET CAMILLE FONTAINE AVEC LA COLLABORATION DE CHRISTOPHER HAMPTON ET JACQUES FIESCHI LIBREMENT ADAPTÉ DE L'OUVRAGE D'EDMONDE CHARLES-ROUX « L'IRREGULIERE » PARU AUX EDITIONS GRASSET & FASQUELLE IMAGE CHRISTOPHE BEAUCARNE A.F.C COSTUMES CATHERINE LETERRIER DECORS OLIVIER RADOT MONTAGE LUC BARNIER MUSIQUE ORIGINALE ALEXANDRE DESPLAT SON NICOLAS CANTIN JEAN-CLAUDE LAUREUX DOMINIQUE GABORIEAU ASSISTANT REALISATEUR JOSEPH RAPP A.F.A.R. SCRIPTE AGATHE GRAU MAQUILLAGE THI THANH TU NGUYEN COIFFURE CORINE MAILLARD COIFFURE JANE MILON DIRECTION DE PRODUCTION FREDERIC BLUM PRODUIT PAR CAROLINE BENJO CAROLE SCOTTA PHILIPPE CARCASSONNE SIMON ARNAL UNE COPRODUCTION HAUT ET COURT CINE@ WARNER BROS ENTERTAINMENT FRANCE FRANCE 2 CINEMA AVEC LA PARTICIPATION DE CANAL+ CINE CINEMA FRANCE 2 EN ASSOCIATION AVEC FILMS DISTRIBUTION COFINOVA 5 BANQUE POPULAIRE IMAGES 9 ET SCOPE PICTURES UNE DISTRIBUTION WARNER BROS

      www.cocoavantchanel.fr

The following year, the French director Anne Fontaine made a biopic that tells the story of Gabrielle before she became an icon of style. *Coco Avant Chanel* narrates her difficult childhood in the orphanage, and her youth up until the time she inaugurated her fashion house. The French actress Audrey Tautou went well beyond the stereotype of the legend, using candor and spontaneity to portray Coco as a woman who also endured pain and tragedy.

Audrey Tautou played the young Gabrielle in the 2009 movie Coco Avant Chanel, *directed by the French director Anne Fontaine. With her slender figure, dark eyes and hair, and delicate face, the actress brought an extraordinary physical resemblance to her role as Mademoiselle.*

Coco Chanel & Igor Stravinsky came out the same year. It was a plunge into the Paris of the 1920s, when the designer's name was on everyone's lips but when, behind the scenes, she was broken as she mourned the death of her love, Boy Capel. Her life was transformed by the encounter with the composer and the passionate bond they developed; a relationship that the lead actors Anna Mouglalis and Mads Mikkelsen interpreted with great feeling.

Between one runway show and another, Karl Lagerfeld adventured into movie making and directed a tribute to the immortal Coco that he presented at the inauguration of the Chanel Métiers d'Art collection in 2013. The Return is a short film dedicated to the reopening of the fashion house in 1954, after the war and her exile in Switzerland, starring Geraldine Chaplin as Coco. In the following years, Lagerfeld directed other tributes, including Once Upon a Time, a black-and-white period film that tells the story of Coco's early years in the boutique in Deauville. He called on Keira Knightley, one of the brand's celebrity muses, to play the young Coco. With the street where the boutique was located in the background with its black-on-white sign, true anecdotes and fictitious conversations play out between the characters who surrounded her during those years, the companions and accomplices of her first successes. Lagerfeld also directed a short film titled Once and Forever, with Kristen Stewart in the role of an actress who was called to play Coco.

Since 2012, the official Chanel website has been releasing short films on its microsite, called Inside Chanel. The series of videos is divided into categories about the history of the brand and stories that are related to it. Much like a potentially infinite strand of pearls, the series is a work in progress that continues every year, visually narrating the landmarks of Coco's personal and professional paths using commentary and previously unreleased materials from their archive, presented with a completely contemporary design and pace.

The actors Anna Mouglalis and Mads Mikkelsen in a scene from Coco Chanel & Igor Stravinsky, *the 2009 movie directed by Jan Kounen.*

Coco's words are at least as immortal as her style. Ironic, blunt, and sometimes biting, they too have become legendary. They still dictate the rules about what a woman should (and should not) wear to be elegant and to avoid going unnoticed. "Fashion reflects the times in which we live. Even if, when times are trivial, we prefer to forget it," she used to say, insisting that luxury was not wealth but a lack of vulgarity.

She was a genius in combining clothing and accessories and often repeated "A woman with good shoes is never ugly," as she encouraged women to take care of themselves. Always. "I don't understand how a woman can leave the house without fixing herself up a little—if only out of politeness. And then, you never know, maybe that's the day she has a date with destiny. And it's best to be as pretty as possible for destiny." It was difficult to disagree with her when she stated "Simplicity is the key to elegance." She was a feminist before the term existed and was famous for her irony about the other sex. "A man can wear what he wants; he'll always be a woman's accessory." Not only did she dress women like goddesses, she told them that to build their character, they needed to learn to use fashion, not endure it. "If there's no woman inside the dress, a real woman, then the dress is useless, whatever it is."

But perhaps her best aphorism, the one that describes her best, was: "In order to be irreplaceable, one must always be different." Exactly like Coco.

On the facing page and on the pages that follow, the shots taken in Paris in 1936 by Boris Lipnitzki for his famous series. Coco was just over 50 and was at the height of her beauty.

Author

Chiara Pasqualetti Johnson is a journalist with a degree in art history. She writes about travel, art, and lifestyle for *Dove* and *Bell'Italia* magazines, as well as for other specialized publications. She has edited books and book series about the history of modern and contemporary art for the publishers Electa and Rizzoli. With White Star, she published *The Most Influential Women of Our Time*, an illustrated volume dedicated to the most influential female figures of the 20th century, which has been translated into six languages.

Bibliography

Vogue on: Coco Chanel, Bronwyn Cosgrave, Quadrille, London 2012 • *Coco Chanel: The Legend and the Life*, Justine Picardie, Harper Collins, New York 2012 • *Sleeping with the Enemy: Coco Chanel's Secret War*, Hal Vaughan, Penguin, New York 2011 • *Coco Chanel*, Linda Simon, Reaktion Book 2011 • *Chanel: an Intimate Life*, Lisa Chaney, Fig Tree, New York 2011 • *Chanel: Couture and Industry*, Amy de la Hay, V & A, London 2011 • *Intimate Chanel*, Isabelle Fiemeyer, Gabrielle Palasse-Labrunie, Flammarion, Paris 2011 • *Chanel, Her Life, Her World and the Woman Behind the Legend She Herself Created*, Edmonde Charles-Roux, MacLehose Press, London 2009 • *Chanel, the Couturiere at Work*, Amy de la Haye, The Overlook Press, New York 2007 • *Chanel: Collections and Creations*, Daniele Bott, Thames & Hudson, London 2007 • *Le temps Chanel*, Edmonde Charles-Roux, Editions de la Martinière, Paris 2004 • *Coco Chanel: Un parfum de mystère*, Isabelle Fiemeyer, Payot & Rivages, Paris 2004 • *Chanel*, Francois Baudot, Assouline, Paris 2003 • *Chanel: joaillerie*, Francois Baudot, Assouline, Paris 2003 • *Memoires de Coco*, Louise de Vilmorin, Gallimard, Paris 1999 • *Les bijoux de Chanel*, Patrick Mauries, Thames & Hudson, London 1993 • *Coco Chanel*, Alice Mackrell, Batsford Ltd, London 1992 • *Chanel: a Woman of her Own*, Axel Madsen, Henry Holt and Co., New York 1990 • *Chanel m'a dit…*, Lilou Marquand, Jean-Claude Lattes, Paris 1990 • *L'irrégulière ou mon itinéraire Chanel*, Edmonde Charles-Roux, Hachette, Paris 1989 • *Journal 1942-1945*, Jean Cocteau, Gallimard, Paris 1989 • *Coco Chanel*, Marcel Haedrich, Pierre Belfond, Paris 1987 • *Chanel*, Jean Leymarie, Skira, Geneva 1987 • *Bendor: Golden Duke of Westminster*, Leslie Field, Weidenfeld & Nicolson, London 1983 • *Misia: The Life of Misia Sert*, Arthur Gold, Robert Fizdale, Macmillan, London 1980 • *L'allure de Chanel*, Paul Morand, Éditions Hermann, Paris 1976 • *Les années Chanel*, Pierre Galante, Mercure de France, Paris 1972 • *Chanel solitaire*, Claude Delay, Gallimard, Paris 1971

Photo Credits

page 5: Granger Historical Picture Archive/Alamy Stock Photo
page 7: Lipnitzki/Roger Viollet/Getty Images
page 10: Horst P. Horst/Condé Nast/Getty Images
page 13: Granger Historical Picture Archive/Alamy Stock Photo
page 15: Photo12/L'illutration
pages 16 and 17: Lebrecht Music & Arts/Alamy Stock Photo
pages 18 and 19: Private Collection
page 20: Fine Art Images/Heritage Images/Getty Images

page 21: Apic/Getty Images
page 23: Roger Viollet/Alinari, Firenze
page 25: Archives Charmet/Bridgeman Images
page 26: Apic/Getty Images
page 27: Granger Historical Picture Archive/Alamy Stock Photo
page 28: Photo12/Universal Images Group/Getty Images
page 29: Bettmann/Getty Images
pages 30-31: Pictures Inc./The LIFE Picture Collection/Getty Images

page 32: Bridgeman Images

page 33: Apic/Getty Images

pages 34 and 35: Brooklyn Museum Libraries, Special Collections/ Bridgeman Images

page 37: Granger Historical Picture Archive/Alamy Stock Photo

page 38: Tallandier/Bridgeman Images

pages 40 and 41: Fine Art Images/Heritage Images/Getty Imagess

page 43: ERIC FEFERBERG/AFP/Getty Images

page 44: Archives Charmet/Bridgeman Images

page 47: Charles Sheeler/Conde Nast/Getty Images

page 49: Time Life Pictures/Pictures Inc./The LIFE Picture Collection/Getty Images

page 50: Granger Historical Picture Archive/Alamy Stock Photo

page 51: Bridgeman Images

page 52: Sasha/Getty Images

page 53: Hulton-Deutsch Collection/CORBIS/Corbis/Getty Images

page 54: Berenice Abbott/Getty Images

page 55: Sasha/Getty Images

page 56: Hulton-Deutsch Collection/CORBIS/Corbis/Getty Images

page 57: FPG/Hulton Archive/Getty Images

page 58: AFP/Getty Images

page 61: Roger Viollet/Alinari, Firenze

page 63: Look and Learn/Bridgeman Images

pages 64-65: ARCHIVIO GBB/Alinari, Firenze

page 66: Hulton Archive/Getty Images

page 69: Bettmann/Getty Images

pages 70-71: Robert DOISNEAU/Gamma-Rapho/Getty Images

page 72: Pictorial Press Ltd/Alamy Stock Photo

page 73: Lipnitzki/Roger Viollet/Getty Images

page 74: George Hoyningen-Huene/Condé Nast/Getty Images

page 76: Moviestore Collection Ltd/Alamy Stock Photo

pages 78-79: Bettmann/Getty Images

page 81: History and Art Collection/Alamy Stock Photo

page 82: Archives Charmet/Bridgeman Images

pages 85 and 86: Lipnitzki/Roger Viollet/Getty Images

page 87: Boris Lipnitzki/Roger Viollet/Alinari, Firenze

page 88: Boris Lipnitzki/Roger Viollet/Getty Images

page 89: Pictorial Press Ltd/Alamy Stock Photo

page 91: akg-images/TT News Agency/SVT

page 92: Granger Historical Picture Archive/Alamy Stock Photo

page 94: KAMMERMAN/Gamma-Rapho/Getty Images

page 95: Gilbert UZAN/Gamma-Rapho/Getty Images

page 96: Granger Historical Picture Archive/Alamy Stock Photo

page 97: Granger/Bridgeman Images

page 98: Ministère de la Culture – Médiathèque du Patrimoine/François Kollar/RMN-Réunion des Musées Nationaux/Alinari, Firenze

page 101: Pictorial Press Ltd/Alamy Stock Photo

pages 102-103: Bettmann/Getty Images

page 104: Lipnitzki/Roger Viollet/Getty Images

page 105: Cecil Beaton/Condé Nast/Getty Images

page 107: Keystone-France/Gamma-Keystone/Getty Images

pages 108, 109, 110 and 111: Boris Lipnitzki/Roger Viollet/Alinari, Firenze

page 112: Horst P. Horst/Condé Nast/Getty Images

page 113: Granger Historical Picture Archive/Alamy Stock Photo

page 114: Boris Lipnitzki/Roger Viollet/Alinari, Firenze

pages 118-119: Granger Historical Picture Archive/Alamy Stock Photo

page 120: Granger Historical Picture Archive/Alamy Stock Photo

page 123: Henry Clarke/Condé Nast/Getty Images

page 124: adoc-photos/Corbis/Getty Images

page 126: Loomis Dean/The LIFE Picture Collection/Getty Images

page 127: SZ Photo/Bridgeman Images

page 129: Horst P. Horst/Condé Nast/Getty Images

page 130: Henry Clarke/Condé Nast/Getty Images

page 132: KAMMERMAN/Gamma-Rapho/Getty Images

pages 134-135: Evening Standard/Hulton Archive/Getty Images

page 136: Suzy Parker/Condé Nast/Getty Images

page 138: Bettmann/Getty Images

pages 140-141: Jack Garofalo/Paris Match/Getty Images

page 142: Lipnitzki/Roger Viollet/Getty Images

page 143: KAMMERMAN/Gamma-Rapho/Getty Images

page 145: Personalities/TopFoto/picturedesk.com

page 146: Granger Historical Picture Archive/Alamy Stock Photo

page 147: Granger/Bridgeman Images

page 148: Cecil Beaton/Camera Press/Contrasto

page 149: KAMMERMAN/Gamma-Rapho/Getty Images

page 150: Art Rickerby/The LIFE Picture Collection/Getty Images

pages 152 and 153: Fabio Petroni

page 154: Gift of Ambassador George Feldman and Miss Margot Feldman from the collection and in memory of Marion S. Feldman/Bridgeman Images

page 155: Gianni Penati/Condé Nast/Getty Images

page 156: Paul Schutzer/The LIFE Picture Collection/Getty Images

page 157: Christie's Images/Bridgeman Images

page 159: BOTTI/Gamma-Keystone/Getty Images

page 160: MediaPunch Inc/Alamy Stock Photo

page 163: Pierre Bernasconi/Apis/Sygma/Corbis/Getty Images

pages 164-165: Douglas Kirkland/Sygma/Corbis/Getty Images

page 166: Douglas Kirkland/Sygma/Sygma/Getty Images

page 167: Douglas Kirkland/Sygma/Corbis/Getty Images

page 168: Douglas Kirkland/Corbis/Getty Images

pages 168-169: Douglas Kirkland/Sygma/Sygma/Getty Images

page 170: Douglas Kirkland/Sygma/Corbis/Getty Images

page 171: Douglas Kirkland/Corbis/Getty Images

page 172: Douglas Kirkland/Sygma/Corbis/Getty Images

page 173: Keystone Pictures USA/ZUMAPRESS.com/Alamy Stock Photo

page 174: Photo 12/Alamy Stock Photo

pages 174-175: Adelaide de Menil/Condé Nast/Getty Images

pages 176-177: James Andanson/Sygma/Getty Images

page 179: PLAINVIEW/Getty Images

page 180: Robert Doisneau/Gamma-Rapho/Getty Images

page 181: Three Lions/Stringer/Hulton Archive/Getty Images

page 182: Musee Carnavalet/Roger Viollet/Getty Images

page 183: Magnum Photos/Contrasto

page 184: The Advertising Archives

page 185: The Andy Warhol Foundation/Corbis/Getty Images

page 187: Ed Feingersh/Michael Ochs Archives/Corbis/Getty Images

page 189: Grzegorz Czapski/Alamy Stock Photo

pages 190-191: The Advertising Archives

pages 192, 194 and 195: The Advertising Archives

page 197: Bertrand Rindoff Petroff/Getty Images

page 198: Foc Kan/WireImage/Getty Images

page 199: Kristy Sparow/Getty Images

pages 200-201: Photo 12/Alamy Stock Photo

pages 202 and 204-205: Horst P. Horst/Condé Nast/Getty Images

page 206: AFP/Getty Images

page 209: Studio Lipnitzki/Roger Viollet/Alinari, Firenze

pages 210-211: Robert Doisneau/Gamma-Rapho/Getty Images

page 212: Bettmann/Getty Images

page 213: AF archive/Alamy Stock Photo

page 214: Photo 12/Alamy Stock Photo

page 215: Entertainment Pictures/Alamy Stock Photo

pages 216-217: AF archive/Alamy Stock Photo

page 219: Boris Lipnitzki/Roger Viollet/Alinari, Firenze

pages 220-221: Roger Viollet/Getty Images

Back cover:
Musee Carnavalet/Roger Viollet/Getty Image

WS White Star Publishers® is a registered trademark property of White Star s.r.l.

© 2020 White Star s.r.l.
Piazzale Luigi Cadorna, 6
20123 Milan, Italy
www.whitestar.it

Translation: ICEIGeo, Milan (editorial coordination: Lorenzo Sagripanti; translation: Cynthia Anne Koeppe)
Editing: Phillip Gaskill

All rights reserved. No part of this publication may be reproduced, stored in a retrieval system,
or transmitted in any form or by any means, including electronic, mechanical, photocopying,
recording, or otherwise, without written permission from the publisher.

ISBN 978-88-544-1740-3
1 2 3 4 5 6   24 23 22 21 20

Printed in Italy by Rotolito S.p.A. - Seggiano di Pioltello (MI)